Take-Down y

A Do-It-Yourself Guide to Building PVC Take-Down Bows, Take-Down Arrows, Strings and More

Nicholas Tomihama

Take-Down Archery

Levi Dream

Copyright © 2012 Nicholas Tomihama

www.backyardbowyer.com

Printed in the United States of America

First Printing in 2012

All rights reserved. No part of this book may be reproduced in any form, by any means including but not limited to mechanical, photographic, or electronic process, or in the form of a phonographic recording, nor may it be stored in a retrieval system, transmitted, or otherwise be copied without permission from the publisher in writing.

This book is intended as an informational guide. The views expressed within are solely the opinions of the author, based on personal experience. All instructions within this book must be followed with caution, and the author, publisher, printer and all other parties involved deny any responsibility for injury to both body and property due to the misuse of information contained herein.

This book is a description of the process the author takes to make simple PVC pipe bows. The results portrayed in the book are as done by the author and are not indicative of work done by other individuals. While the information is presented in a clear and concise manner, the author makes no guarantee that following the instruction will yield the same quality work. Nor does the author, publisher, printer and all other parties involved suggest following the instructions within as they carry risk inherent to all forms of archery and the bowyer's craft.

Bows are inherently dangerous weapons and care must be taken during the use and manufacture of them. No bow is indestructible and every bow, regardless of strength can hurt, maim or kill. Never point a bow at another person, animal or into a place that may not be clear. Only use safe equipment when practicing archery. All minors must be supervised by a responsible adult.

ISBN : 978-1479348480

For Angie, Levi and Noah

He that giveth heed unto the word shall find good;
And whoso trusteth in the Lord,
happy is he.
- Proverbs 16 : 20

Table of Contents

Chapter One - Getting Started   6
    PVC Bow Anatomy   6
    How a PVC Bow Works   7
    Selecting PVC Pipe   11
    Finding Your Measurements   14
    Arrows and Archer's Paradox   17
    Strings   21
    Safety and Precautions   23

Chapter Two - Tools   26

Chapter Three - Taper Flattening   29
    Flattening Jig   30
    Heating Trough   35
    Making a Bow Blank   38

Chapter Four - Egyptian   50
    Initial Tuning   51
    Shifting Center   55
    Reflexing and Deflexing   59
    Making and Attaching Siyahs   62
    Fine Tuning   69
    Three Piece Take Down   71
    Finishing   72

Chapter Five - Tracker   77
    Initial Tuning   78
    Shaping Nocks   80
    Fine Tuning   84
    Two Piece Take Down   86
    Four Piece Take Down   90
    Finishing   93

Chapter Six - Nomad   95
    Initial Tuning   96
    Making and Attaching Siyahs   98
    Fine Tuning   103
    Three Piece Take Down   105
    Finishing   109

Chapter Seven - Arrow Rest   111

Chapter Eight - Release Aid   118
    Design   119
    Building   120
    Shooting   124

Chapter Nine - Take Down Arrows   129
    Carbon and Aluminum   130
    Wood   134
    Fletching Jig   138
    Fletching An Arrow   144

Chapter Ten - String Building   151
    Serving Jig   152
    String Jig   157
    Endless Loop   160
    Center Serving   173
    Setting a Nock Point   175

Gallery   178

Glossary   184

Bonus Track   187
    ABS Stalker Quiver   187
    Screw-In Wood Adapter   194

Chapter One
Getting Started

Welcome to *Take-Down Archery*! We'll be going over some of the basic parts of a bow, how PVC take down bows work and some things to think about before building your own equipment. By the end of this book you should be able to put together an archery kit that is effective, safe and can be packed down into a backpack or bag. We'll start with some bow anatomy.

PVC Bow Anatomy

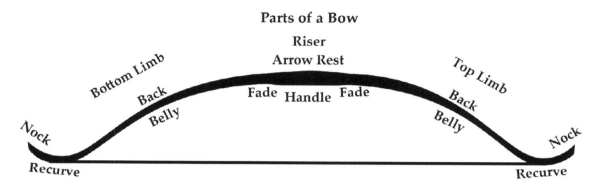

The types of bows in this book are simple and while they may each look a little different, they all have the same parts. The main body of the bow is broken up into three main parts. They are the riser, limbs and ends of the bow.

The riser is located in the center of the bow and consists of the handle and fades. The handle is the are where the hand grips the bow and the fades are the transition or fade from limb to handle. An arrow rest, which is where an arrow sits when the bow is in use, is located on the handle.

The limbs are the part of the bow that do the most work and take up the most space. There are two separate limbs, one upper and one lower. Each limb has a back, which faces away from the archer when the bow is held and a belly, which faces the archer when the bow is held. We'll go over the importance of the back and belly in the next section.

At the end of each limb are the bow's nocks and the limb tips. The limb tips may be recurved, which means the string curls over the limb when the bow is strung. If the string touches or rests only on the string nocks, the bow is not considered a recurve. The nocks are where the bow string sits, effectively connecting the ends of a bow.

Bows can come in many shapes and most can be described in a few simple terms. A reflex is any curve in a bow that curves away from the archer, while a deflex curves toward the archer. A recurve is essentially a hard reflex at the tip of a bow. Reflex and deflex can happen in different places in the same bow. Next we'll go

Getting Started - How a PVC Bow Works

over how these things plus some other aspects can make a bow that performs well.

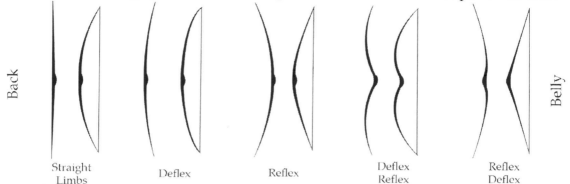

Some different bow shapes. The bows in this book use combinations of reflex, recurves and deflex in order to bring out the most in each.

How a PVC Bow Works

When it comes to a simple bow, efficiency is all about energy storage and transfer. An efficient bow is able to put the most energy into an arrow with minimal input. While the idea of PVC bows usually evokes images of pipes with strings on them, a bow made in this way will not be very efficient.

A bow is essentially a spring. When the bow is drawn back, energy is stored. When the string is released, energy is released. In order to work well, a bow must be able to store a large amount of energy and then release most of it into the arrow.

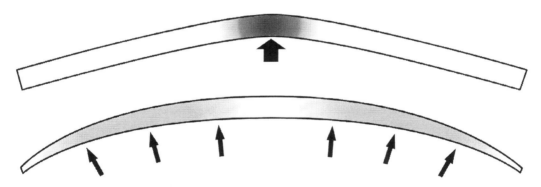

The top bow flexes mainly in the middle because it is essentially a straight stick of equal strength along its length and is not very efficient. The bottom bow gradually reduces in strength from handle to tip and is very efficient.

A bow that is equally strong along its entire length, much like a straight stick or a PVC pipe, will flex the most in the middle when strung. This happens because the act of stringing a bow pulls the limbs backward and inward. If the whole bow is equally strong, something has to give and the middle is put under the most strain. Because PVC pipe is so flexible, it can work this way. Most other materials would break under such strain.

A bow that flexes only in one spot, while it can store a great deal of energy, cannot release that stored energy easily. Most of it feeds back into the bow. So while a bow like this can store energy, its inability to use it effectively lowers the amount of energy it can make use of. If the bow is able to flex in more than one place, it is able to release that stored energy better.

A simple way to understand this is to imagine if you were holding two 10 foot long poles. Trying to swing those forward, like they were bow limbs, would be very difficult to do. In the end, you would expend a lot of energy and the poles would move very slowly. Now if you cut each pole into ten pieces and had nine other people with you, each person could swing their arms very quickly. Put together, the same distance would be traveled with less strain on the individual and with more speed.

Most traditional bows work in this way. By spreading out the strain, these bows are able to store and release energy efficiently. Traditional bows achieve this by reducing the amount of material as you move from handle to tip. This can be done by removing more material from the tip than the center or adding more material near the center of the bow.

With a PVC pipe bow, which is essentially a hollow pipe, these things cannot be easily done. Instead, there is a little trick that can mimic the effect of less material by progressively weakening the pipe.

A cylinder gains strength from its circular cross section. This cross section makes it stable in all directions equally. Yet if the shape is compromised and the cylinder flattens to an oval cross section, it will be stronger in one direction than the other. By manipulating this, a bow can be made from PVC pipe that is stiff in the handle with limbs that flex evenly.

If a pipe is flattened with a taper, starting thickest at the handle and then getting flatter toward the tips, the same flex of a traditional bow is replicated. A taper flattened PVC pipe can be formed in to many shapes, including reflexes and recurves. Because it is so flexible in the direction it was flattened, it is equally as rigid in the other direction. From side to side it is very inflexible and therefore stable.

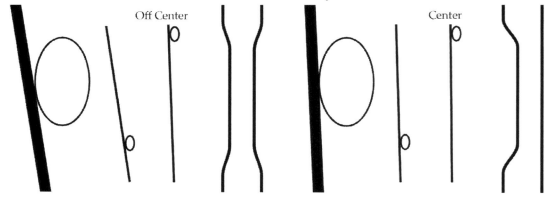

Because it is so stable, it can resist twisting. This ability can be utilized to make the bow more forgiving to shoot. In the diagram above, you can see the bow on the left side has a nice and centered handle. If an arrow is placed on the string, it has to go off at an angle to avoid the handle like in the first picture. As this bow is drawn back like in the second picture, the angle decreases until the arrow is almost pointing straight at the target.

When the string is released and the arrow flies, the string will want to travel

Getting Started - How a PVC Bow Works

straight. Because the angle constantly gets wider as the arrow gets pushed further forward, the string and arrow fight each other. The string will oscillate from side to side as the arrow gets pushed into the handle of the bow and deflects off.

After driving into the bow and trying to fold around it, the arrow will rebound and flex outwards, then flex back around the handle of the bow. If the arrow is just flexible enough to yield but stiff enough to recover, it will straighten out and fly true despite its turbulent launch.

Because taper flattened PVC bows can be so stable, the handle can actually be shifted to one side like the bow on the right. When an arrow is nocked, the angle is much less pronounced. At full draw, the arrow nearly makes a straight line to the target. When the string is released, it does not need to fight the arrow as much and the arrow does not drive in to the bow as hard.

As a result, the arrow leaves the bow cleaner with less initial turbulence and only needs to flex from side to side a little to correct itself. The string also travels in a straighter path. This all works together to maximize the amount of energy that goes into the arrow's flight. An arrow from this bow does not need to be as perfectly matched and may even benefit if it were on the stiff side. An arrow also needs less in the way of fletching to stabilize in flight.

Now that our PVC bow is both efficient and consistent, we need to find a way to break it apart while still allowing it to function. The simplest way to do this is to cut the bow in half and reinforce the handle with a sleeve of some sort. The pressure of the bow string pulling the limbs inward and backward keeps the handle from coming apart when the bow is strung and shot.

This works because the handle section of such a bow should not flex. Because there is no flex, the handle simply needs a strong and rigid connector or support that can resist the pull of the bow at full draw. This is the most common way to make a bow into a take down version and has been done for centuries. While this yields a very portable bow, it is still half the length of a bow and can still be too long to pack in a backpack or bag.

A more modern take down system that is only decades old is a 3 piece version. A bow like this consists of a rigid and large riser section and two limbs. Because the bow is in three pieces it packs down smaller, despite having a larger and bulkier riser. PVC bows can be made in this way, but a simpler and very effective method is to make use of PVC's flexibility.

There are very few take down bows that actually work with bending sections of limb. The simple reason for this is that a bow is a very balanced and stressed object. Under normal circumstances, a bow strung and drawn is under enough stress that any rigid connections on the limbs could cause the bow to fail on either side. If the connector flexes as well, it may snap at the connection or slip out at full draw. The general rule is to keep any connection as stiff and stable as possible and this can usually only be achieved right off a rigid riser.

Because PVC is so flexible, it can be held together with an adequately long sleeve made of a larger diameter of PVC pipe. Simple friction and the inward pull of the bow on itself keep the connectors together. These connectors give just enough flex to the bow, coupled with just enough stiffness to allow them to work. The connectors work with the bow's limbs, allowing even mid-limb connections to work without fail.

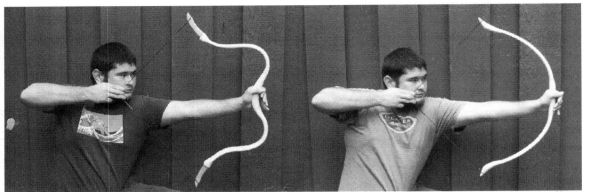

The bow on the left is a poor candidate for mid-limb connectors because the pressure of the string pulls straight back in the crucial areas. For the bow on the right, the inward tension would keep mid-limb connectors secure.

Only certain designs work well with mid-limb connectors for the simple reason that too dramatic of a bend in the wrong direction could cause the limbs to pull apart at full draw. Mid-limb connectors work best on bows that are slightly reflexed or at least have no added curves in the middle of the working limb. If there is too much of a deflex like the bow pictured above left, the limbs would pull out and could hit you.

This is compounded by the fact that the inward pressure, which normally helps keep the bow together, would in this case help in loosening the limb connectors. On the other hand, most bows will work well with a handle connection as the handle is almost always under a lot of inward pressure. When making any bow with connectors, make sure that they are never drawn past their maximum draw length or the pieces may pull out and go flying. This can be very dangerous.

Finally in regards to the shape of the bow, placement of reflex and deflex can give the bow different qualities. Reflexes, even slight ones, help to stiffen an area of the bow. They also help present the bow's tips forward of the handle, which increases the amount of stored energy a bow can use. Deflexes usually increase the softness of the bow, making areas that are deflexed more yielding and able to bend. Deflex, along with string follow works to reduce the overall amount of stored energy a bow can use.

Set is a term that relates to a permanent bend of a bow. When a bow has been in use for a time, and this is particularly true of PVC pipe, it will take a great deal of set or bend towards the belly of the bow. Set is a type of deflex. When set causes the tips of the bow to fall behind the handle, it is called string follow or following the string.

If you have two bows, one highly reflexed and one deflexed, the reflexed bow will make use of more energy. This is because while both bows may have the energy capacity, there is only so much distance a bow can be pulled back. A bow that is reflexed is under much more strain than a bow that is deflexed or has string follow. This strain is similar to the bow being drawn.

Getting Started - Selecting PVC Pipe

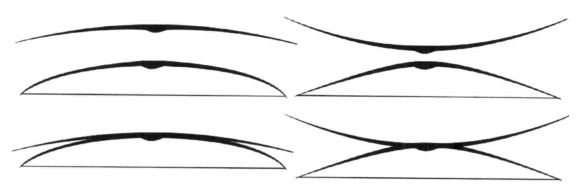

The bow on the left is deflexed and the bow on the right is reflexed. Notice the difference in limb position from unstrung to being strung. This difference gives a good idea of the extra energy pre-loaded into the bows' limbs.

If you take a look at the two bows above, you will notice that the bow on the left shows very little difference between being strung and being unstrung. Because of this, most of the energy this bow can store and use will come from the draw. This bow will return to its resting shape very slowly as there is very little strain on the bow's limbs.

The bow on the right is under much more strain. The further a bow's tips sit in front of the bow, the faster the bow will want to return to rest when fired. In a way, it's as if the bow is already drawn before the bow is drawn. A deflexed bow, if brought to a very high brace height, will behave similarly when strung. Recurves usually allow an otherwise deflexed bow to gain some degree of reflex.

Now that we have a basic understanding of how to make a good PVC bow, let's go over what makes good quality PVC pipe.

Selecting PVC Pipe

PVC pipe, while common all over the world, is extremely varied in its formulation and composition. This can make finding suitable pipe for bow-making difficult. Add to this several other types of plastic commonly sold in place of PVC and it can get very confusing.

The PVC pipe I use and get the best results from is schedule 40 PVC pressure pipe. This is a common pipe sold throughout the US for plumbing. I use white pipe that is no more than a year old in manufacture. Due to the constant changing of standards and the practice of storing PVC pipe outdoors, it's always a good idea to choose the newest pipe possible.

In the US there are several types of PVC pipe, the but ones to use are schedule 40 and schedule 80 pressure pipe. Stay away from cellular core, SDR, drainage, electrical conduit and non rigid piping. These are all inadequate for making bows and will likely fail or produce a frail or very slow bow.

Cellular core pipe is piping with a foam-like structure valued for being light and will not be able to withstand the stresses of a bow. SDR graded pipes are usually much thinner than their schedule counterparts as they are rated on pressure rather than wall thickness. Most SDR pipes will be well below 1/8 of an inch thick and border on 1/16. In metric, these pipes are usually around 2 mm in thickness.

Take-Down Archery

3/4 Inch SDR-21

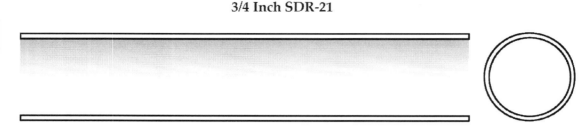

    Drainage, electrical conduit and non-rigid PVC are not designed to be under pressure. Because of this, their formulations usually make them softer and more flexible than white pipe, which is quite rigid and brittle as far as plastics go. These tend to make bows that are slower and deform very quickly.

    Schedule refers to pipe thickness. 40 is a lighter, thinner pipe that is often white to off-white in color. This is the most common sort of pipe available in the US. Its thickness will be near 1/8 of an inch thick for 1/2, 3/4 and 1 inch pipes. 1 inch will be a little thicker. For metric piping exported from the US, the wall thickness will be near 3mm.

3/4 Inch Schedule 40

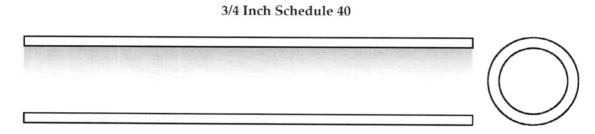

    Schedule 80 is a thicker, heavier grade of pipe used for plumbing. While a dark gray color is usually standard for most manufacturers, there are some white pipes available. White pipes tend to be more rigid than their gray counterparts. Gray PVC is more resistant to UV degradation, so if you don't plan on painting your bows, the carbon black added to gray pipes may be extra assurance. Schedule 80 pipes are roughly 5/32 of an inch thick or around 4 mm for metric piping.

3/4 Inch Schedule 80

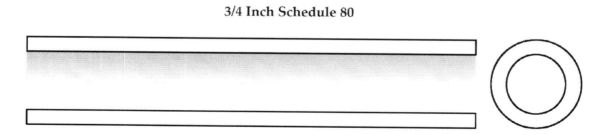

    The bows in this book use schedule 40 pipes. Schedule 80 pipes tend to drive up the poundage of the bows and require longer pipe to start with. They are less likely to collapse but more prone to break if over-stressed.

    PVC pipe in the US is of a very high purity and is quite clean as far as

Getting Started - Selecting PVC Pipe

PVC goes. Many toxic fillers and stabilizers have been replaced with more inert ingredients. Most pipe made to US standards are composed mostly of pure PVC polymer resin, which is a whitish powder that is composed of stable polyvinyl chloride, a polymer of vinyl chloride monomer, a fairly toxic gas. The next main ingredient is a filler, usually calcium carbonate in the form of chalk powder. After this, stabilizers and plasticizers are added. In the US, toxic stabilizers like lead and toxic phthalates have long been taken out of PVC pipe manufacture. Exact formulation depends of the manufacturer.

By law, PVC pipes must have the date of manufacture as well as the schedule and pressure rating. For reference, schedule 40 pressure ratings are around 600 PSI for 1/2 inch, 480 PSI for 3/4 inch and 450 PSI for 1 inch. For schedule 80, it's 850 for 1/2 inch, 690 for 3/4 inch and 630 for 1 inch pipe. These should be on the outside of any new pipe and are one more way to distinguish between pipe ratings.

With US standard PVC pipes, it's a good idea to first make sure the pipe is not too old. Most of the time, PVC pipes are stored outdoors. Now, PVC like any polymer can be degraded by UV light. UV light and burning PVC pipe release chlorine gas and slowly cause PVC to lose its flexibility as the polymer bonds break apart. While this sounds terrible, it's a very slow process and is usually a problem if PVC is kept outdoors in the elements nonstop for 2 years.

That said, it is always good to buy fresh pipe as the stress of flexing and recovering will push PVC beyond the normal pressure cycles it was designed for. New pipe can be white to an off, eggshell white. This depends on how much titanium dioxide is present in the pipe and differs from manufacturers. New PVC pipe can be fairly lustrous or have a chalky feel, either one is fine. Though the shinier pipes will usually be more flexible than chalky pipes. Before using them, always wash pipes inside and out with warm soapy water to remove any debris or contaminants from storage and manufacturing.

If PVC is old or getting brittle due to too much exposure to heat it will begin to turn yellow. SDR pipes are often yellow in color because the thin pipe is much more susceptible to UV damage than thicker pipes. Excess fluctuations in temperature can also cause hairline cracks to form in PVC as extreme cold causes the plastic to turn brittle. Pipes stored in excess cold can have very thin spiderweb-like cracks. Try to lightly flex every pipe before using it as these cracks can hide until the bow finished.

When purchasing and using PVC pipe outside of the US, keep in mind that formulation is varied and properties are affected by formulation. The majority of developed nations have stepped up safety regarding PVC piping by either phasing it out or switching to safer ingredients. Always use caution when buying pipe in other countries and take extra steps to protect yourself.

Some pipes are still produced with known cancer-causing plasticizers and heavy-metal stabilizers. Some pipes, especially in less developed nations, use varying grades of ingredients and may contain unpolymerized vinyl chloride monomer. These carcinogenic substances can be released in the form of gas or vapors when these pipes are heated.

Aside from health risks, pipes not manufactured to a rigid standard can be inconsistent in internal thickness and stability. Pipes made in other countries have a tendency to be more brittle and prone to breakage, which can be dangerous. Where US pipe will fold or have clean, fairly crumbly edges, many foreign pipes can shatter into multiple razor-sharp shards much like glass.

Because most developed countries are banning all PVC plasticizers, a great deal of available PVC pipes are called UPVC or unplasticized polyvinyl chloride. Again, it's difficult to say exactly how these pipes will all fare because each manufacturer follows a different recipe. Some are exceedingly brittle and won't stand up to the stress of being a bow, some are too soft and fold frequently or are very weak and others work perfectly.

In some countries, other plastic pipes have replaced PVC for most uses. If the variety of PVC pipes is staggering, then the variety of other plastic pipes available will inundate you. If all you have is other plastic pipes, experiment. Always use caution, wear full eye and lung protection and be smart. While some plastic pipes may or may not work, the basic principle of taper-flattening can be applied to any hollow pipe if adapted properly.

Now that you know what to look for, let's go over finding your bow and arrow measurements.

Finding Your Measurements

It's important before making a bow or buying arrows for yourself that you know a few measurements. The first important measurement is draw length, which is the distance you will draw the bow back when you shoot. There are a couple methods to estimate your draw length and give you a general idea of where to start.

First, measure your wingspan. Stand against a wall with your arms spread out on either side and have somebody measure that distance. Alternatively you can use your height, as both height and wingspan are roughly the same for most people. Take this number, subtract 15 or the width of your chest between shoulders, and divide that by 2.

The resulting number should be close to a normal draw, which is limited by the length of your bow-holding arm. Another way to measure this is to hold your arms straight out in front of you with both hands together and fingers pointing forward. The distance between your fingers and chest will be around your length of draw. A similar method is to measure from your armpit to the second joint of your index finger.

This length is based upon drawing the bow to your face or chin. This is a good area to draw to as it brings your eye in line with the arrow and keeps you from overextending. Another way to draw a bow is to draw to the cheek or lower jaw which can add an extra inch or so to your draw length. Either one will work, it's mostly personal preference.

The best way to measure draw length is to draw a very light bow with an arrow. If you have someone to help you, draw the arrow until you are in a comfortable position, and have your assistant mark where the arrow meets your bow-holding hand. Make sure they are not in front of the arrow when doing this. If you are by yourself, tie a piece of string loosely onto the arrow. As you draw the

Getting Started - Finding Your Measurements

All draw length/weight combinations in gray could be dangerous as they over-stress the bow and may cause any limb connectors to pull free at full draw.

PVC Pipe Recurve Weight in Pounds for 1/2 Inch Pipe

Pipe Length	Draw Length in Inches				
	24	25	26	27	28
50	5-10	10	10-15	15	15-20
49	10	10-15	15	15-20	20
48	10-15	15	15-20	20	20-25
47	15	15-20	20	20-25	25
46	15-20	20	20-25	25	25-30
45	20	20-25	25	25-30	30
44	20-25	25	25-30	30	30-35

PVC Pipe Recurve Weight Chart in Pounds for 3/4 Inch Pipe

Pipe Length	Draw Length in Inches				
	26	27	28	29	30
50	25-30	30	30-35	35	35-40
49	30	30-35	35	35-40	40
48	30-35	35	35-40	40	40-45
47	35	35-40	40	40-45	45
46	35-40	40	40-45	45	45-50
45	40	40-45	45	45-50	50
44	40-45	45	45-50	50	50-55

PVC Pipe Recurve Weight Chart in Pounds for 1 Inch Pipe

Pipe Length	Draw Length in Inches				
	26	27	28	29	30
60	35-40	40	40-45	45	45-50
59	40	40-45	45	45-50	50
58	40-45	45	45-50	50	50-55
57	45	45-50	50	50-55	55
56	45-50	50	50-55	55	55-60
55	50	50-55	55	55-60	60
54	50-55	55	55-60	60	60-65

bow back, the string will catch on your hand and travel up the arrow, marking your draw length.

For example, my calculated draw length is 27 inches. Drawing to my chin, I draw just under 27 inches. Drawing to my cheek, I pull 28 inches. Drawing to the back of my jaw, I pull 29 inches. The bows in this book are laid out for an archer with a 28 inch draw. If your draw length is more or less than 28 inches, add or subtract 1 inch of bow length for every inch of draw.

It is important that when you are finding draw length you give your bow a little more length than you think you need. It's very easy to draw an inch too far if you get really excited

The next measurement is draw weight, or the amount of force required to draw a bow back to full draw. We will measure draw weight in pounds, meaning a bow that is 40 pounds is equal to lifting 40 pounds when the bow is fully drawn. To measure the weight of a bow, a pull scale can be used to measure the bow at full draw. In lieu of a scale, the tables on the last page will give you a rough idea of draw weight at different lengths based on starting pipe lengths. These charts are only a guide and only apply to PVC bows made using the techniques in this book. Be careful. The shorter the bow, the higher the chances that it could fail. If making a take down bow, too short a bow may pull free from the connectors at full draw.

Draw weight is a little trickier to calculate than draw length. Unlike length, draw weight is determined by both the inherent strength and physical condition of the archer. A bow's weight is essentially the amount of force it takes to pull and hold it at full draw. It's tempting to start heavy. If you aren't already used to archery, pick a lower draw weight to start and then work your way up. If you build your first bow long it can be shortened to increase weight.

Draw weight varies from person to person, though a person's weight is a good general indicator. If figuring out weight for yourself or someone else, here's a simple chart to get a general idea of where to start.

Archer Weight to Bow Weight in Pounds

Weight of Archer	50-70	70-100	100-130	130-150	150-180	180+
Bow Weight	5-10	10-15	15-25	20-35	30-50	40-65

The chart above is very rough, though it is a good place to start. It's best to make a couple bows and use the one that is most comfortable for you. If a certain weight becomes too light for you, these bows can be shortened to bring the weight up. Just work an inch at a time.

If you are an experienced compound archer, keep in mind that these bows draw differently and should be roughly 10 to 15 pounds lighter than what you are accustomed to. These bows are at their peak weight at the end of the draw. All of their weight is exerted completely at full draw.

Keep in mind that archery, especially during practice, should be more of an aerobic exercise. The lighter your bow, the more repetitions you will be able to do and the longer you will be able to hold your draw before getting exhausted. Try not

Getting Started - Arrows and Archer's Paradox

to draw a bow that will tire you quickly as both accuracy and consistency will suffer.

There are particular styles of archery that specialize in the use of heavy bows from 70 to over 200 pounds in the extreme. Such archery requires much training and proper form to avoid irreparable damage to your joints. Be careful and never draw more than you are comfortable with.

Now we'll talk about arrows and how they help complete an archery setup.

Arrows and Archer's Paradox

Arrows are one of the three main parts of a bow setup. You have the bow itself, a string and the arrow. Arrows are important. A good arrow can make a bad bow alright and make a good bow perform even better. First we'll go over what happens to an arrow when launched from a bow and how to stay safe while still getting good performance.

Because of its length, an arrow is a dynamic thing. While it may be hard to see when shooting, an arrow does not merely travel in a straight line. When a arrow is released, the front and rear of the arrow are in conflict with each other. The point of the arrow, which is at rest and not moving, wants to stay at rest. The nock of the arrow, which is being pushed by the string and is in motion, wants to stay in motion.

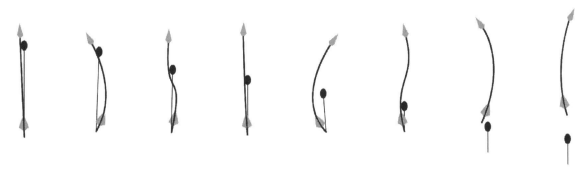

An illustration of an arrow as it is fired from a bow. The bends are exaggerated to show the dynamic movement of an arrow in motion. The bow handle is an oval and the string is represented by a straight line.

The arrow immediately begins to flex as the rear of the arrow pushes forward while the point stays in place. This happens very quickly and soon the arrow acts like a spring itself and pushes the point forward. This kicks the whole arrow into motion. If you shoot with fingers, the string will actually twist and force the arrow to flex toward the bow harder. At the same time, the string gets kicked out away from the bow handle.

As the string drives the arrow forward, the point starts to flex in the other direction toward the bow. Since the handle is in the way and the arrow cannot simply oscillate now, the middle of the arrow seemingly wraps around the bow handle. This is one area where spine, or the stiffness of an arrow, is vital to safety.

Once the arrow has flexed enough, it more or less clears the handle and straightens out, though the point is still curving to the handle side of the bow. Now that the handle is out of the way, the arrow flexes in the opposite direction and the string swings over to the other side. This curve is uninterrupted because there is

Take-Down Archery

nothing to impede the arrow's flex.

Once the string stops moving, the arrow jerks as it breaks free from the string. While this is happening, the arrow is already trying to flex the opposite way. This time the handle is in the way again. The front of the arrow flexes away from the bow handle while the rear of the arrow snakes around the bow handle. At this point, the string makes a final jerk away from the handle, one of the potential causes of wrist slap.

With the arrow now free of the bow, it flexes back and forth in flight. Its oscillations quickly diminish as the fletchings take over and stabilize the arrow. Instead of traveling straight along the bow in the direction it is aimed, the arrow ends up travelling straight along the path of the bow string. This happens because the string is what directs the arrow and the arrow will do its best to follow that direction.

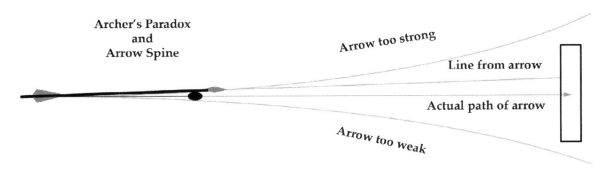

Archer's Paradox. When a properly spined arrow is fired from a bow, the arrow does not travel along the line where the arrow itself points, but rather along an imaginary line that follows the path of the string to the target.

This is known as the Archer's Paradox or just Paradox. It would make sense that an archer aiming his bow at a target with the arrow off to one side should not be able to hit that target. By reason, the archer should aim slightly off to the side to line the arrow to the target. The paradox comes in because an archer aiming with his bow and not his arrow will hit his mark while an archer who aims with his arrow will miss.

Now this paradox only comes in to play on bows where the arrow does not line up with the target at brace. With a bow that allows an arrow to sit in-line with the string, the arrow will line up with the string and there is no Archer's Paradox involved. Paradox also only happens when an arrow is of the perfect balance of stiff and flexible, or perfectly spined to the bow.

A properly spined arrow, meaning one that is flexible enough to curve around the bow yet stiff enough to return true, will follow the path of the string consistently. If the arrow is too stiff or strong, it will go off to the side of the bow it is sitting. This happens because the arrow drives into the bow handle and bounces off rather than flex around it. If an arrow is too weak, it will wrap around the bow too much and end up traveling off to the side of the handle.

If a bow's handle sits in the middle of the string's path, the arrow needs to

Getting Started - Arrows and Archer's Paradox

flex quite a bit to get around it and recover. Back in the second section we went over how PVC bows can have their handles moved to one side. By doing this, the effect of Paradox is lessened greatly. This is because there is much less difference between the path of the string and the direction an arrow points at full draw.

Because the effects of Paradox are lessened, finding your arrow's spine is much easier. The exact effect of spine on an arrow depends on two main factors. First, the closer to center the arrow sits the less paradox there will be as the arrow will not need to flex around a side handle. These arrows can be made stiffer as they don't need to flex as much. Secondly, different materials react differently in terms of recovery.

There are a variety of arrows that are available in many different materials. One of the oldest and most traditional arrow materials is wood. Wooden arrows are relatively heavy and are somewhat forgiving of spine. While wood works well, it is hard to find consistent arrows made of wood just because wood is a natural material. The most common wood used in arrows today is Port Orford Cedar, a softwood prized for its strength and straightness. While wood is forgiving, it is much more likely to break than other materials at the proper spine.

Aluminum arrows have been the standby for many years. They are made of very thin-walled aluminum alloy tubes. While they are manufactured with very close tolerances and are very straight, aluminum arrows are less forgiving when it comes to spine. The plus side is that every arrow in a matched set will be close to being the same as every other arrow. This allows consistency from shot to shot. Aluminum arrows are very durable and when they break they snap or fold rather than splinter.

One of the newest arrow materials is carbon or carbon fiber. Composed of strands of carbon or graphite suspended in a synthetic resin, carbon arrows are incredibly stiff and light. One of the benefits of carbon arrows is that they stabilize much faster than wood or aluminum. This makes arrows accurate and consistent over a range of spines. The main drawback is that if they ever break they splinter, creating a puff of razor sharp carbon fibers along the break.

Aluminum and carbon arrows also have the added benefit of being impervious to humidity and temperature. Differences in temperature and humidity will affect how a wood arrow will flex, possibly making them less consistent. Wood arrows also tend to lose their stiffness after many repeated shots.

When buying arrows, ask for spine charts. Manufacturers usually have charts that let you get a rough idea on how to match an arrow at a certain length and point weight to your bow. When dealing with spine, the longer the arrow the weaker it is and the heavier the point the weaker it is. An arrow spined for 25-30 pounds and then cut down to 24 inches with a light target point is stiffer than an arrow spined 45-50 pounds but 34 inches long and with a 125gr. field point.

If you buy arrows, make sure they are of good quality. Research the manufacturer or maker and if you make them yourself, don't rush or cut corners. Some archers give up the sport after an arrow breaks. It's that jarring and frightening. Always inspect arrows before shooting them. Flex them in your hands and if they creak, make noises or crack, don't shoot them.

Take-Down Archery

The main thing to pay attention to when purchasing arrows is what they are fletched with. Fletching is the arrow's method of guiding and steering. Feathers have been and are still preferred by many archers as they are very forgiving to shoot and lighter than plastic vanes of a similar size. Plastic vanes can also be used on arrows.

I suggest using arrows fletched with feathers as these bows are shot off the hand or a shelf. Feathers will lies flat when pressed and then spring back when pressure is released. When the feathers pass over your hand or shelf, they fold down and then come back to stabilize the arrow.

Plastic vanes on the other hand don't fold flat down, they ripple and fold to either side as the arrow passes over. This can cause the arrow to kick off from the shelf, making it harder to stabilize. Over time the vanes can get rippled from repeated use and the rippled vane will affect the arrow's flight as it gets more and more distorted.

Plastic vanes are lower maintenance and are less likely to be ruined by moisture and mud. Feathers require more maintenance. If they get really wet the web will bunch up and the arrow will not fly as consistently. The feathers will need to be steamed gently and then dried quickly. There are some plastic vanes available that mimic feathers enough to make they work better than other plastic vanes for arrows shot on the shelf. If you are using a flip style rest, shooting vanes are less of a problem.

When it comes to turning your arrows into take downs, there are a couple things to keep in mind. The first thing is that an arrow is, as we've seen, dynamic. It doesn't just lurch forward like a thick and inflexible spear. Rather, it flexes and flies through the air gracefully toward its mark. An arrow's flex is a big part of designing a take down arrow.

When designing a take down arrow, it's important to realize that the area of most stress is right in the center of an arrow. Take down methods should be planned accordingly.

In this book we cover two basic methods of converting an arrow into a take down version. In the picture above, the top method is an external sleeve for wood arrows and the bottom is a screw and insert connection for aluminum and carbon arrows. There are other methods of making take downs and other orientations as well, but these are the safest for the material and style.

When an arrow flexes, it bends right in the middle, much like a bow without a taper to it. More than any part of the arrow, the very center of its mass will be

Getting Started - Strings

under a great deal of stress. Yet it is this part of the arrow which has the most flex and avoids bow contact the most.

Wooden arrows can be easily converted into a take down version with a stiff sleeve of brass or aluminum that slides over the cut shaft. While this style of arrow can be cut in more than one place, a 2 piece arrow is better for a few reasons. First, because the arrow flexes the most in the center, placing non-flexible connectors on either side of the center would simply increase the strain the arrow is under. By placing the connector on this area of great stress, some of that strain is relieved.

Secondly, the center of the arrow avoids the bow the most as it whips from side to side. This allows a connector that is proud, or does not sit flush with the rest of the arrow, to pass over the bow with minimal contact. This helps keep the connectors from deflecting the arrow off the bow.

Finally, the extra strain on the connector actually forces the two halves of the arrow together. This can help prevent a connector slip which could cause the arrow to pull apart. It is very important that the arrow stays intact, as the shorter end of the arrow could easily drive into your arm or bow hand if the connection fails. Connectors on either side of the center are more likely to fail than one directly on center.

On the other hand, screw and insert connections are better in a 3 piece configuration where the connectors are away from the center. Screw and insert connections are only as strong as the screw holding the pieces together, so this style of joint needs to remain as unstressed as possible.

Because the connection is flush with the arrow pieces, it is alright if the connectors contact the bow. They do not sit proud and will not interfere with the flight of the arrow. By keeping these weak spots away from the center, some strain is actually drawn out to the rest of the arrow. In a way, this style of connector is very similar in function to the sleeve connector.

Always remember to check an arrow before and after shooting. If there is any problem at all, do not shoot the arrow. A broken bow may hit you in the head or body, though usually won't have any lasting effects. A broken arrow could cripple your arm, hand or eyes for life, so be careful and always check arrows every time.

Now let's complete the set and talk about strings.

Strings

Selecting bow strings is an important and often overlooked aspect especially with PVC bows. The string is just as important as any other part of a bow. In order to get the most out of your PVC bow, a properly matched string is vital. Here are a few ideas that will help when selecting strings.

A bow string is what transfers energy from the bow into an arrow. By pulling the string back, an archer loads energy into the bow's limbs. At the same time, energy is being loaded into the string as well. If the string is too weak and cannot handle the stress of being under pressure, it will break and feed what energy was loaded into the bow back into the bow's limbs. The string will also try to release its energy and could cause injury.

If a string is strong enough but too stretchy, it will absorb more energy than

Take-Down Archery

it should when the bow is drawn. This means that there is less energy stored in the bow's limbs. When this happens, efficiency is reduced.

When the string is released and the bow's limbs begin to snap back, the energy that was loaded into them goes back into the string. Since a good string can't hold much energy, the string begins to put it somewhere. If there is an arrow on the string, the string puts energy into the arrow and the arrow will accelerate. If there is no arrow on the string, the string will feed the bow's energy back into itself.

If the string is too weak, it will break just as the arrow leaves the bow and any residual energy in the limbs feeds back into the string. If it is too flexible, the string will absorb more energy when the bow snaps back. As a result, less energy goes into the arrow and the arrow travels slower. Once the arrow leaves the string, a stretchy string will give under the residual energy of the bow's limbs. This dissipates energy and may cause the string to hit your wrist even if the brace height is high.

When selecting a string for your bow, you want to find a string that is strong but not very stretchy. Most commercial recurve strings are made with either Dacron or low-stretch and low-creep materials like Fast Flight and Dyneema.

Dacron is a polyester, low stretch and strong. It does stretch a little, making it more forgiving on the bow while still offering lots of performance. The other blends are designed for speed and consistency. These produce a very strong and light string that uses energy more efficiently and won't stretch from the weight of a bow.

PVC bows will work with both Dacron and modern string materials. Because modern strings have almost no give to them, string nocks need to be padded with leather or rubber to prevent the string from cutting through the nocks.

There are two different types of string commercially available. The first is called a continuous loop or endless loop string. It is a strong design that lessens string creep and stretch and offers a little more speed. This is the style we'll be building in chapter 10. The second is called a Flemish twist or Flemish splice. It is often seen on selfbows and longbows and is quieter though often a little slower than endless loop strings.

While both have their own strengths, both will work for a string. Really it just comes down to your own personal preference.

Commercial strings are sold either by the length of the string itself from loop to loop or based on a standardized measure for bow length. To find both, you need to measure your bow. Your bow's effective length, or nock to nock length (ntn), is the distance from one nock to the other. Use a piece of string to measure from one string nock, across the contour of the limbs and to the other nock.

This measurement will be used in place of an AMO bow length or string length. If you find strings sold by their own length, take your bow's ntn measurement and subtract 3 to 4 inches. While not perfect, this will get your string in the general size range that can be adjusted.

If you are buying a string for a bow before building it, one way to figure out the finished ntn length would be to start with your bow's starting pipe length. Subtract about half an inch for flattening and then however far away the nocks are from the ends of the bow. So a bow that starts out with a 48 inch pipe and nocks cut 3/4 inches in from the end will be about 46 inches ntn and use a 42 to 43 inch string.

Getting Started - Safety and Precautions

It's always good to know how to build strings, so if you feel like making your own, there are many material options. Modern materials like Dacron and Fast Flight work well, as will alternative string materials like Dacron fishing line, spectra fishing line, dyneema dental floss and so on. Even silk or linen heavy shoemaker's thread will make a fine string.

Now that we have an idea of what string are and how they work, let's go over some safety.

Safety and Precautions

Building PVC bows is a safe and rewarding hobby, but like anything else it has its risks. Like we covered earlier, PVC is polyvinyl chloride. PVC is a thermoplastic, meaning that it can be formed and molded when heated and returns to normal when cooled. PVC itself is made of vinyl chloride monomer, a colorless and odorless gas. While VCM is toxic and cancer-causing, most if not all modern PVC pipes from developed nations are very stable.

When working with US-made PVC pipe, there are few risks. PVC pipe is inert and the stabilizers and fillers used in modern pipe are all very stable, even when heated. The main danger comes from overheating, melting or burning PVC pipe. When burned, dioxins and chlorine gas are released. Because of this, always work in a well ventilated area and wear if a respirator for organic vapors. Chlorine gas forms hydrochloric acid when it comes in contact with water, so do not inhale PVC fumes or get too close to burning pipe.

Always be sure that when working with PVC, it never gives off an odor. Proper heating of PVC pipe will not release any odor. If there is an odor, stop immediately and get to fresh air. While safe for adults, heating and grinding PVC can be hazardous to pregnant women, children and developing youth.

Keep in mind that while US pipe is safe to work with, pipes from other countries may contain cancer causing phthalates and heavy metals that could cause developmental and mental illness. Always take extra precautions when working with foreign pipe and be sure to keep any dust off your skin as some lower quality pipes can leach dioxins and vinyl chloride monomer.

Be safe when heating PVC as it can cause burns if it comes in contact with skin. Always be aware of your surroundings and keep your workspace clean and ordered. It's very easy to lose track of where things are, and things like pliable, near-molten plastic or red-hot heat gun nozzles have a way of reaching out and touching you if you aren't sure where they are.

Always wear protective gear when working with hot PVC pipe. Work in a well ventilated area and wear a respirator if possible. A respirator is a must for sanding and cutting PVC pipe. Wear eye protection as well as heat-resistant gloves. It's also a good idea to wear long sleeves, long pants and covered shoes. A thick jacket can help prevent arm burns. Also keep any long hair out of the way when working with heat.

As with any bow, PVC bows are weapons and should be treated with respect. Any bow can fail, and while PVC bows are more resilient than most, never abuse your bow. Abuse or neglecting your bow could cause it to fail which may injure

Take-Down Archery

you and those around you. Always make sure bystanders are a safe distance away and behind you when shooting any bow. It's also a good idea to wear eye and head protection during a bow's break in period, which is around 50 shots after the bow is first built and 50 more after beiong made into a take-down.

Never fire a bow without an arrow on the string. Never point a bow at another person, animal or object of value. Always unstring your bow and keep it in a cool, dark place when not in use. If you treat your bow with respect and build it, shoot it and maintain it with care, it will reward you with many years of service. Treat it like a fine bow worthy of respect and it will be. Treat it like a cheap toy to be beaten and abused and then fail, it will do that too. The same can be said for any wood bow as well.

Like all-wood selfbows, PVC loses flexibility when it gets cold. As the temperature drops, the plastic will become less forgiving. It can take a great deal of practice before a stable shooting cold weather bow can be made as it takes a feel of the material to get it to perform. If shooting in temperatures below freezing, try to keep the bow as warm as possible. And before shooting, take a couple half-draws to help get the bow used to bending again.

As an additional note, PVC gains speed and power as the temperature goes down. By shortening your draw an inch or so, you can retain the same speed and power as full draw in warmer climes. I find that my range of motion is also limited when it is very cold, so a shorter draw comes naturally to me. Keep in mind that if you are in a usually-cold environment, you may benefit from using gray pipes, which usually have lower stiffness but a more flexibility at lower temperatures than white pipe.

As far as storing and using your bow, remember than this is a working, almost living object. It is dynamic and moves, flexes, accelerates and stops. It is a powerful tool and needs to be taken care of. Keep it in the same temperatures you like to be in, don't expose it to the elements or outside where you wouldn't be comfortable. Especially if you build a bow, no matter the material, it is a part of you. Don't let anyone else draw your bow unless you are sure they know how to. They may injure themselves or others if they are unaware of the limits of your personal bow and shooting style.

PVC can be broken down, like all polymers, by UV light. Over time, exposure to UV light can cause the plastic to become brittle and it can break if strung or drawn. One way of knowing if a pipe is UV damaged is it will appear yellow compared to new PVC pipe. Regardless of the finish you choose or if you want to show off the raw PVC pipe, UV blocking is important. There are a few quality plastic spray paints and clear coats that have UV blockers. I always apply this under a wrapped or glued on finish and over any painted or dyed finish.

Finally, when building your equipment, make sure it is your best work. When working with arrows, make sure that your start with quality and put quality work into them. Arrows are under a lot of stress, especially if they are already compromised with take down connectors. Always make sure your arrows are in perfect condition before shooting. Never assume they are fine because they shot well before. Each shot is a life-altering event for an arrow and you never know when one

Getting Started - Safety and Precautions

may snap.

     The same goes for a take down bow. Since you've taken a working bow, cut it apart and then put it back together, it may come apart unexpectedly. Always work a bow fully before cutting it apart, as any major fixes cannot be done after connectors are put in place. After every shot, visually inspect to make sure the bow is not pulling out of the connectors at all. If the connectors slip while the bow is being drawn, you could hit yourself in the head or body and may hit yourself in the face with your drawing hand.

     Be safe and always work with caution. Now we'll take a look at some tools and equipment we'll need to start building.

Chapter Two
Tools

While building PVC pipe bows isn't incredibly tool intensive, there are a couple of tools that are needed. At the heart of it, only a heat source, flattening jig and a cutting tool are needed to make a dependable and serviceable bow.

Here are a few basic groups of tools that are very useful as well as some that can easily make the work go very fast. The most important tool, a heat source, can be found in most homes or can be easily obtained inexpensively. All the other tools can be found used or new as well as improvised.

When building the different jigs for strings you will need an electric drill or drill press to make holes. A drill also makes boring the hole in release aids much easier.

Keep in mind that tools of any kind can be dangerous, so be careful. When heating pipe, work in a ventilated area. It also helps to wear an organic vapor respirator. Always wear a dust mask when cutting or sanding PVC pipe and use gloves when working with heat or sharp tools.

Heat Source

The first and most important tool you'll need is a heat source. It will be used for flattening and forming PVC. It can also be used to tweak and fix your bow later when its being broken in and adjusted.

A heat source can be just about anything that gives off at least 300 degrees F. The most controllable are heat guns (rated to at least 1,000 degrees F) and cook-tops whether they be gas or electric. Torches, grills and open fires can also be used, but extra care needs to be taken to avoid burning the pipe. Filling the pipe with hot sand or immersing in boiling water work very quickly but these are very dangerous methods.

Chapter Two - Tools

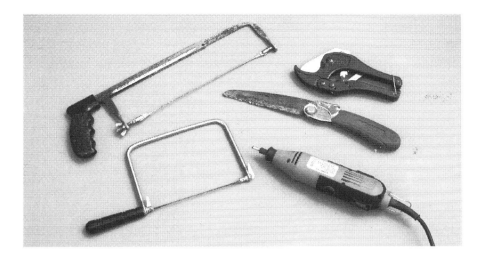

Cutting

PVC is an easy to cut material, so most saws and tools for wood or metal can also be used on PVC. A saw or PVC cutting tool like the one above will be used to cut lengths of pipe as well as for minor clipping and shaping of nocks and PVC pieces.

The saw at the top is actually a tile saw, a carbide coated metal wire in a hacksaw frame. This type of saw is ideal for PVC as it does not clog and it can be used for everything from cutting lengths, cutting tapers, forming all types of nocks and used as a file for rough work. A rotary tool can be used for similar applications.

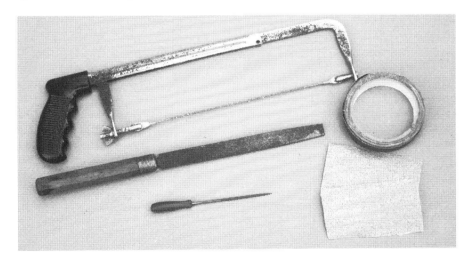

Grinding and Shaping

Files and sandpaper are invaluable for shaping nocks, points and tapers. They will even help make quick work of flattening edges of arrow rests and such.

A tile saw or nock file will be used to cut string grooves in nocks. A nock file is simply a rat-tail or round file that is about 1/8 of an inch in diameter. Sandpaper can be rolled up into a 1/8 inch thick tube as a substitute for a tile saw or nock file.

Power Tools (Optional)

Here is a picture of my most-used power tools. The band saw on the left is used for everything a fine saw could be used for. The miter saw is used almost exclusively for cutting lengths of pipe and occasionally for cutting angles for nocks. The little belt sander does all the rough grinding and sanding work.

While I use these tools often enough to mention them, they aren't needed. Most of the work I do is done with hand-tools anyway. Always wear a respirator and eye protection when using power tools on PVC as they generate heat and produce fine dust.

Chapter Three
Thickness Tapering

The first design element that really sets all these bows apart from being a simple PVC pipe with a string is the taper in the limbs. In chapter one we went over how a bow that flexes in many places is more efficient than one that does not. In a PVC bow, thickness tapering is key. It is also what makes mid-limb takedown sleeves possible.

This chapter goes over a couple tools that make flattening and shaping PVC pipe simple as well as how to actually taper the thickness of a bow's limbs. The first is the flattening jig, the main tool to getting a smooth taper. The second is a heating trough which is a heat reflector that makes heating PVC much more efficient.

At the end, we'll also go over correcting a collapsed bow limb, which is a common problem when first building PVC bows. Keep in mind that even heating is very important and burning or melting sections of pipe may cause them to collapse or snap. Remember to go slow and always keep your heat source moving.

Flattening Jig

The key to getting optimum performance out of a single length of PVC pipe is by flattening the bow into a smooth taper. A flattening jig is an accurate and simple method of getting that clean taper. This jig is just one of many variations that can be done.

It's my favorite style of jig as it allows the pipe to be heated and flattened on the same surface. Using a rigid board also allows the jig to be clamped, allowing for repeatable results every time.

The jig is simple, a longer 2x4 on the bottom with a shorter 2x4 on top. A spacer block in between ensures that the handle section of the bow is thicker than the rest of it. Once a heated pipe is placed in the jig and weight or pressure applied, the angle the spacer block makes ensures an even taper.

The jig itself can be modified and adjusted to make it easier to use. The shorter and longer side can be separated if the single long jig is awkward or takes up too much space. If cutting the jig in half or only building one half of the jig, the jig can work with or without the flattening board. To do this, heat the pipe on a flat surface like a floor or workbench and then place the jig base on top of it, upside down.

Start with a 2x4, 8 feet long. Make sure the board is straight and free of any large knots or holes. Small or dense knots are okay. Cut off one 3-foot length, leaving the other length 5 feet long. The longer board will be the jig base and the shorter board will be the flattening board.

Thickness Tapering - Flattening Jig

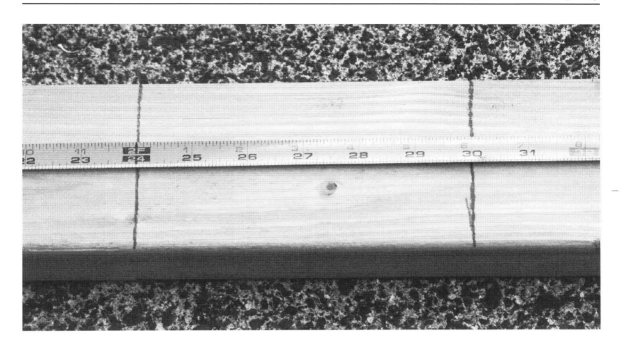

From one edge (it doesn't matter which), measure 24 and 30 inches. Mark a line at each measurement. You will use these to line the pipe up to the jig when flattening.

Here's what the board looks like now. The 30 inch mark should be the center point of the board.

Cut four spacer blocks. The shorter blocks should be roughly 3/4 inches wide and deep and exactly 3/4 inches tall. Place these on the 24 inch mark side. The taller blocks should also be 3/4 inches wide but 1 inch tall. Place these on the 30 inch mark side.

Glue the blocks into place. Make sure the taller blocks are on the longer side and the shorter blocks are on the shorter side. Keep them on the inside of the lines.

Thickness Tapering - Flattening Jig

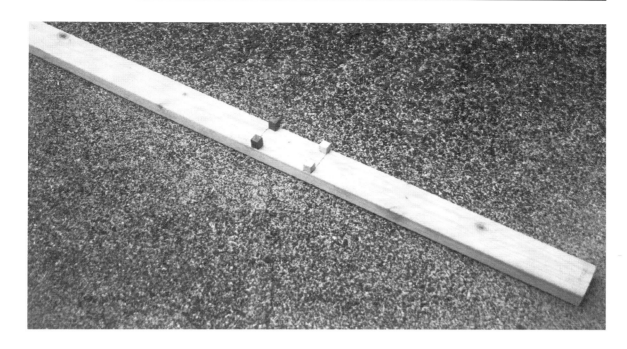

Here's the finished base of the flattening jig. It gives a nice solid base for heating and forming bows as well.

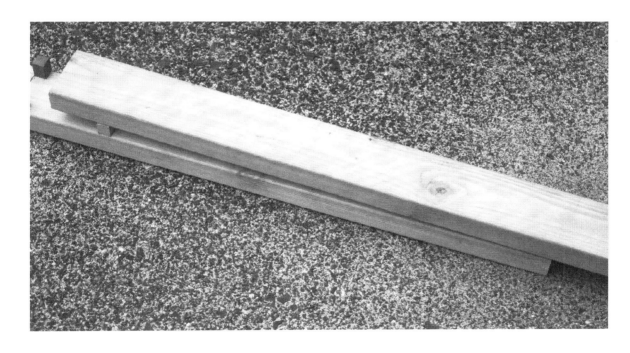

To use the jig for flattening 3/4 inch pipe, place the flattening board on the shorter side.

Take-Down Archery

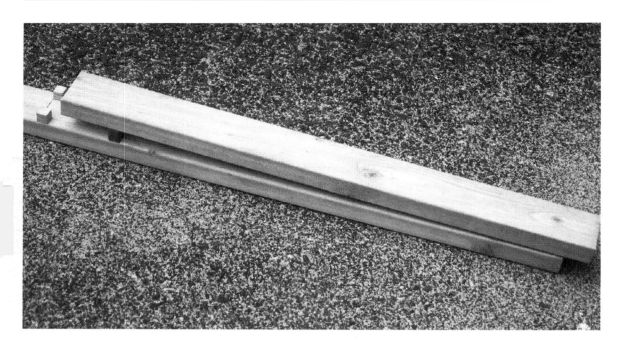

When flattening 1 inch pipe, place the flattening board on the longer side.

Heating Trough

When using a heat gun or other directable heat source, its efficiency can be increased with a heating trough. A heating trough is a channel or half-tube covered with a lining that can reflect heat. This helps retain the heat from a heat gun or other directable heat source, making heating much more efficient.

While not required, this extra tool makes things go a lot faster. In the best of conditions and in a mild temperature, heating a bow limb can take as little as a few minutes. In bad conditions, it can takes an hour or more and that still may not be enough.

The trough keeps heat in and distributes enough heat through the whole trough to keep the entire pipe warm indirectly. It can also aid is preventing plastic burns because direct heat is being drawn around the pipe and not right on it.

This also helps prolong the life of your finished bow, because the less it is heated over and over again, the better it will be.

When using a heating aid like this, be sure to constantly check the pipe, as the pipe could start melting from the accumulated heat. If the pipe ever starts losing its cylindrical shape on its own, the pipe it too hot.

Once the pipe is hot enough to where finger pressure can smash it down, it can be placed in the flattening jig,

We'll be building the heating trough with half a cardboard mailing tube, though any heat-resistant tube would work. The tube should be as long as half of the longest bow you plan to make. It's better to make it too long than too short. For example, a 5 foot long bow needs at least a 30 inch trough.

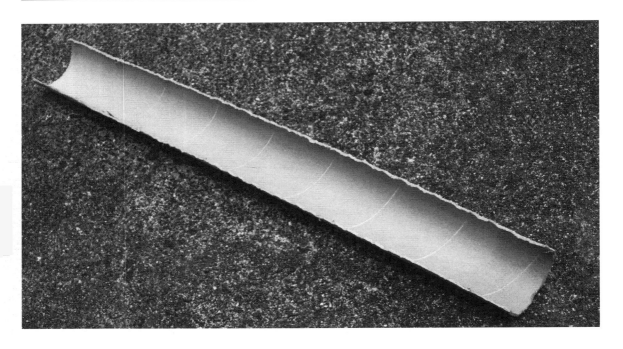

To start, cut the tube in half lengthwise. This will give you an adequate reflective surface and two usable troughs. For more efficient heating, cut a 1-2 inch strip from the top of the tube rather than half. This will allow for faster heating and slower cool-down.

Cut a length of aluminum foil or flashing to fit the tube. It should be wide enough to cover the surface of your trough or tube.

Thickness Tapering - Heating Trough

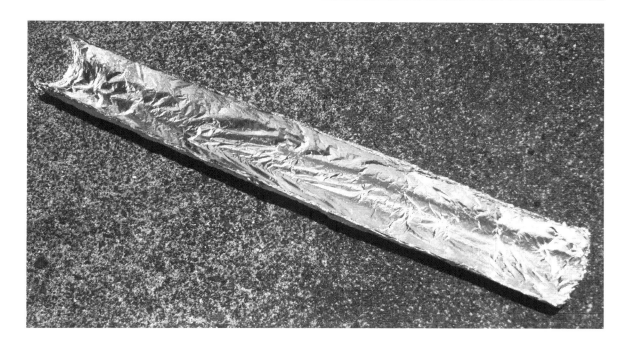

Secure the reflective surface to the tube. This can be done by either crimping the edges over the tube, with staples or other fasteners.

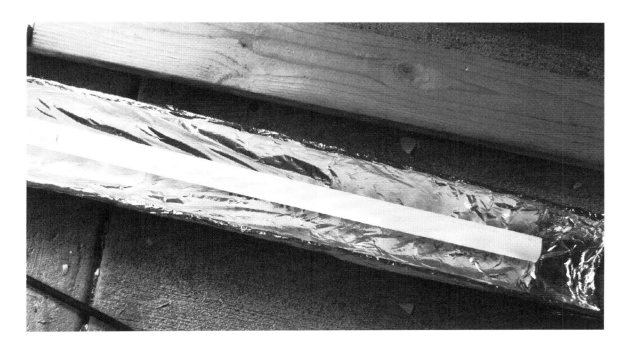

To use the trough, place half of your PVC pipe into the trough and heat it gently is passes with a heat gun or torch. Concentrating the heat on the reflective liner and not the pipe itself, the heat wraps around the pipe and helps lessen the risk of burnt plastic.

Making a Bow Blank

The flattening jig and the general guideline of flattening the limbs to the same as the bow's inner diameter do a few subtle things. First, they lower the potential strength of the bow by reducing stress more than is absolutely necessary. If the bow is kept thicker throughout, more power can be obtained.

Yet by weakening the whole bow it is made more resilient and resistant to breakage than if it were being pushed to its limits. This also allows the handle to be made considerably thicker and therefore stiffer than the rest of the bow. This helps lower handshock and virtually eliminates the chances of the handle breaking by moving the point of weakness away and into the limbs.

This method of flattening also sets the stage for any additional adjustments. A bow straight off the flattening jig will work much like a longbow with almost all of the bow working. From here the bow can be made thinner or thicker in places to increase or draw out strength allowing this simple form to be modified into almost any historical or imagined configuration.

With the bow marked, begin heating one half of the pipe from past the center mark to the tip to prepare for flattening. One method for heating, which works well for any stationary heat source like a stove top or an open flame, is to pass the pipe slowly over the heat source.

Keep the pipe moving to avoid burns. If burns do form, leave the area to avoid exposure to fumes. Always keep the pipe moving as even slight burns could break the bow.

Thickness Tapering - Making a Bow Blank

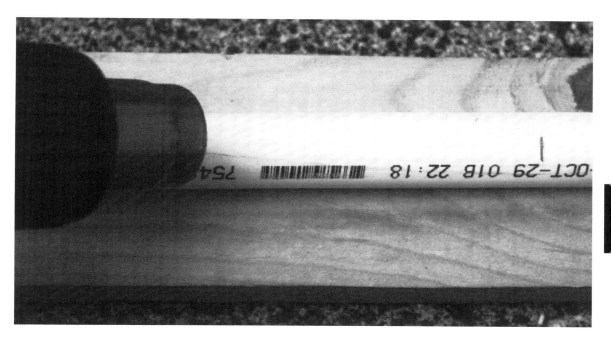

Another method, which works well for directable heat sources like heat guns and torches, is to pass the heat source over the pipe. Using a heating trough is best, though wood or a heat reflective surface also works.

Pass the heat source over the pipe, turn the pipe a 1/4 turn and repeat.

Once the pipe starts to droop like this, it is getting close to being soft enough. At this point, be very careful as touching the soft pipe can cause painful burns. If you need to handle the pipe, use heat resistant gloves or a hot pad.

Keep heating the pipe until you can flatten each section with hand pressure.

Take-Down Archery

Once the pipe is soft enough that every section can be flattened with light pressure, it is ready to be placed in the jig. Line the outer handle mark, the one 3 inches from the center of the bow, with the line on the jig. Make sure the pipe is straight.

Quickly place the flattening board onto the pipe. The flattening board will start at the center mark of the handle in order to maintain an even taper. If the pipe is soft enough, it should take only fifty pounds of pressure to flatten. This can be done by standing on the flattening board or using clamps. While the clamps in the picture are hand clamps, screw-type clamps allow more pressure to be applied.

Thickness Tapering - Making a Bow Blank

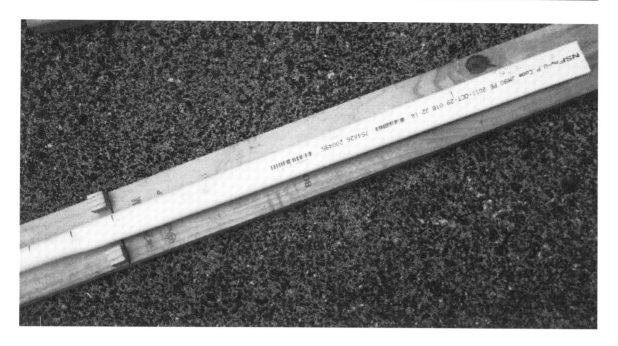

After the pipe has been allowed to cool, remove the flattening board. There should be a steady taper from the center of the bow to the tip. If there are any uneven spots or the back looks wrinkled, reheat the limb and clamp it again.

From the side, this is the proper taper. The tip should be noticeably flatter than the handle in a smooth taper. If the bow is completely flat or the tip is thicker than the handle, the bow will be too weak and may break. If this happens, reheat the limb and re-flatten. The very ends of the tip should just touch together. The rest of the bow should be completely hollow.

Take-Down Archery

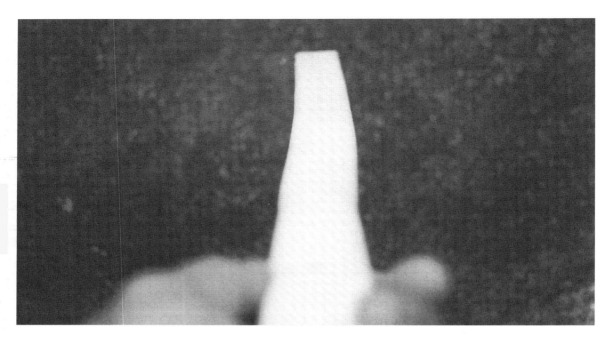

Sight down the limb of the bow. Most times, the limb will be a little crooked. Find the area that is bending the most. In this case, it's the section near the center on the handle side.

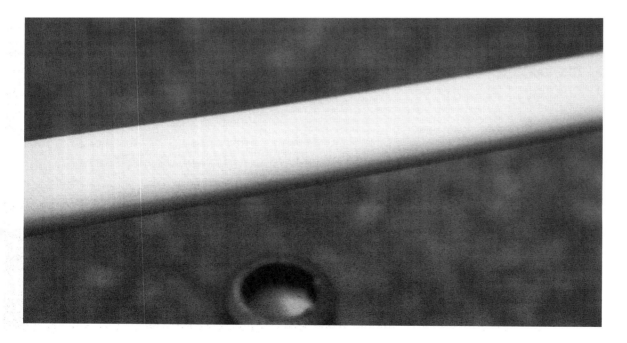

Heat the crooked area of limb gently and evenly. The pipe will become slightly pliable before it begins puffing back up to its original shape. Right when it is soft enough to bend, flex it gently against the curve to straighten the limb. If the limb does start to deform, place it back into the flattening jig after ensuring it is straight.

Thickness Tapering - Making a Bow Blank

This amount of crookedness is acceptable. PVC is very forgiving of slight imperfections. It is not important for the handle to be straight now as that will be fixed next. Just make sure that the limb itself is mostly in-line with itself.

With both limbs flattened, pass the handle section over your heat source. Heat the entire handle section plus one inch over on each side evenly until the pipe returns to its original shape.

Take-Down Archery

Once it is soft enough, the handle will revert to this shape. It may take a little time, but just keep the pipe moving and don't hold it in one spot for too long. Burns in the handle will weaken the bow and may cause it to break. Gentle heating here is important.

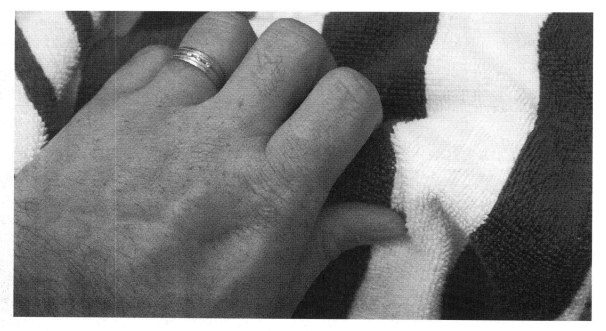

Once the handle is flexible, press the handle from the sides while the pipe is on a flat surface like a board. This gives the handle a more comfortable grip while also strengthening the handle and reducing its ability to flex. Keep pressing and moving as the pipe will want to spring back. Once it begins to set, check it to make sure it's shaping up properly.

Thickness Tapering - Making a Bow Blank

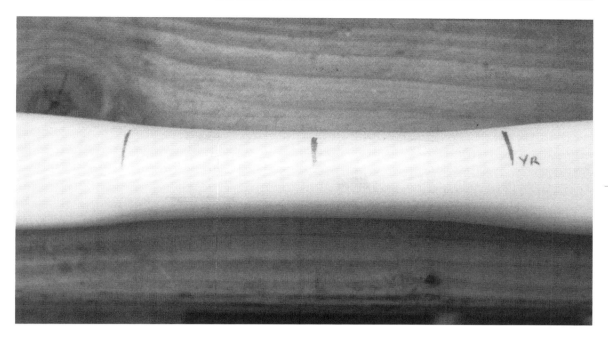

From the back side, you can see the difference in width from the handle to the limbs. The handle section should be fairly uniform with a gentle taper for about an inch on both sides. The handle should be about 1 inch wide.

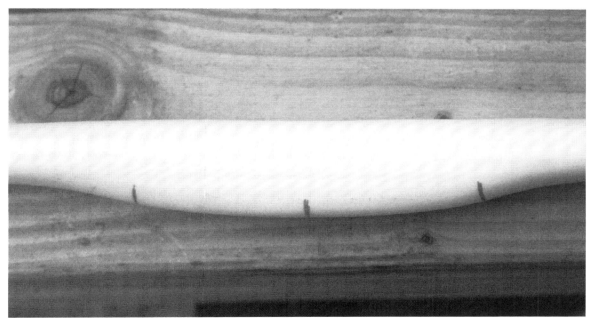

When pressing the handle into shape, be sure to keep even pressure and not press too hard at the edges of the handle. You want a smooth transition from handle to limb like the picture above. If there is a sharp crease here, the handle could fold when the bow is strung up or drawn. If there are any creases or if the handle does fold over, just re-heat the creased section gently and re-form it. Re-forming pipe will not weaken it if done gently.

Take-Down Archery

Once the handle sets but the plastic is still slightly soft, sight down the bow like this. If the handle wasn't straight or if the limbs were twisted before, you can correct this now by flexing the handle gently until the limbs line up.

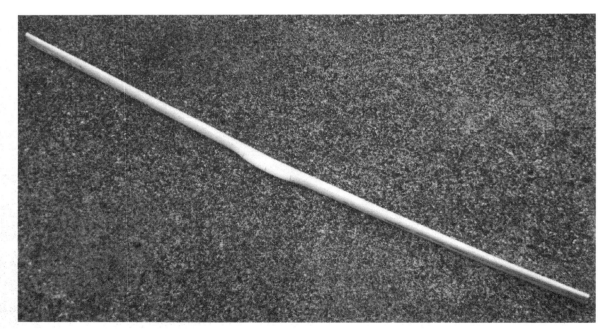

Here's the bow after flattening and handle shaping. From here we will shape the bow into its different variations. If you want to try your own variations on bow shape, this is the base shape to build upon. If strung up now, the bow would be a forgiving and sweet shooter.

Thickness Tapering - Making a Bow Blank

For 1 inch pipe, heat and flatten in the same manner as the 3/4 inch pipe. The heating will take longer as the pipe is not only longer but also larger in diameter. Use the taller flattening blocks on the longer side of the flattening jig.

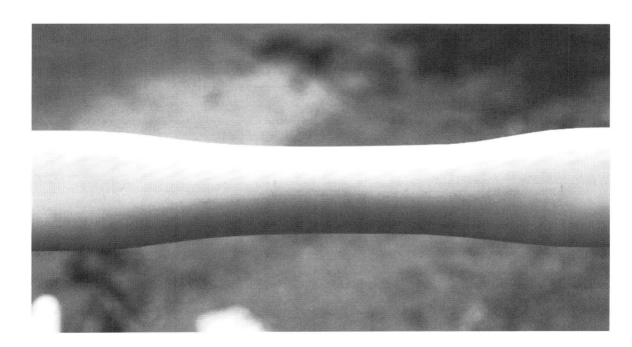

Heat and flatten the handle sideways against a flat surface. The handle should be around 1 and 1/4 inches wide.

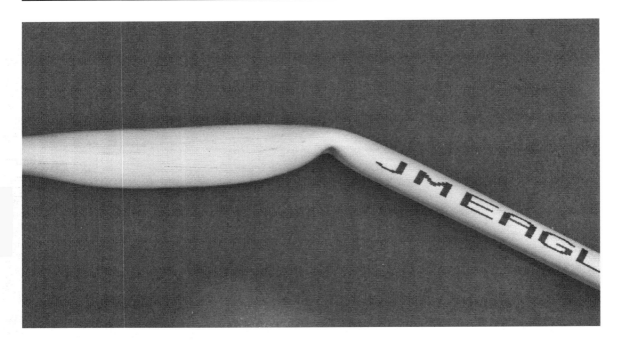

Sometimes when working with PVC, a limb may collapse. This can happen near the handle fade or out on a limb. If this happens and there are no burns or melted areas, it can usually be fixed. Don't try to repair the limb if there are cracks or tears in the plastic.

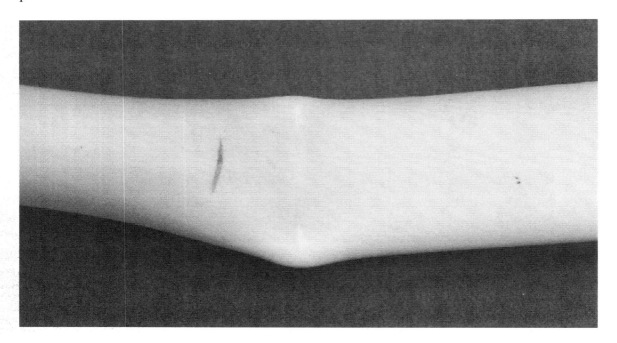

Here's a close up of the collapse. There may be some discoloration, but as long as there are no tears, this can be fixed.

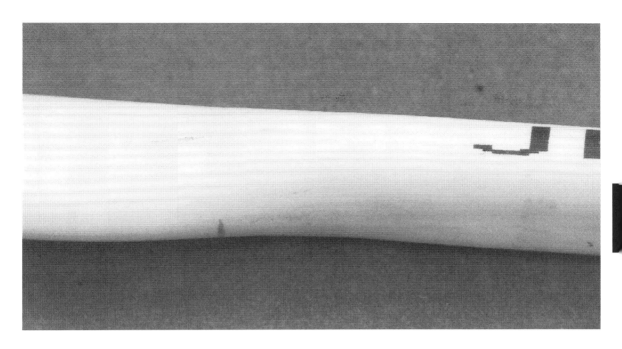

Gently heat the collapsed section until it puffs out. Keep heating until it comes back to normal, then take it off the heat and let it expand a little more. If the discoloration from earlier has gone away, the bow can be used.

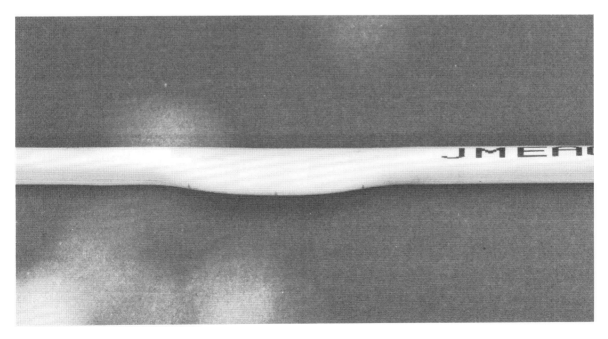

Here's the fixed limb. Make sure the collapsed area is left a little thicker to compensate for the weakness that made it collapse in the first place. Collapses become more common as the bow is made shorter. Once the bow cools, carefully string and test the bow at half-draw before shooting normally.

Chapter Four
Egyptian

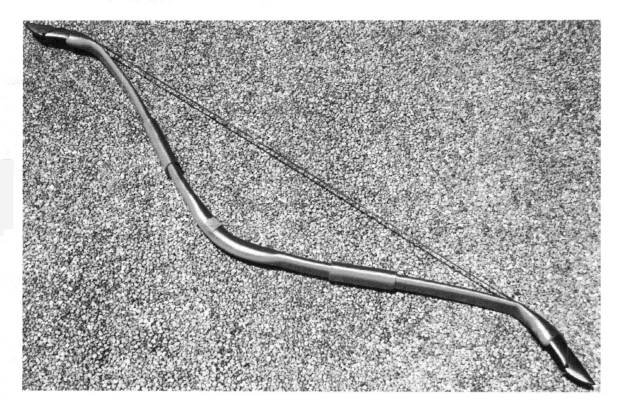

    This bow's triangular shape while braced, sweeping reflexed limbs and hard-deflexed handle are inspired by the reflexed composite bows of ancient Egypt. This combination of reflex and deflex allow this little bow to draw a full 30 inches. It is short, but its recurves and reflex make it almost the same length strung and unstrung.

    In this chapter we'll be going over some different methods of shaping a bow including inserting PVC siyahs or bow ears, reflexing, deflexing and handle shaping. This bow is made for a 28 inch draw and is safest at that length when broken down. Because of its unique shape, this bow lends itself well to a 3-piece take down configuration.

    The bow's limbs are connected in two places with 1 inch pipe as connectors. It is a very stable bow and very smooth in the draw. Its deflexed handle lowers stress while its reflex and recurves help bring up speed. While not particularly powerful, this bow makes a fun backyard shooter which breaks down small enough to keep in the car or take on trips. And while light in the draw, it's still powerful enough for grislier tasks.

Follow the steps in chapter 3 and flatten a 3/4 inch schedule 40, 48 inch long pipe. Use a 3/4 inch spacer block.

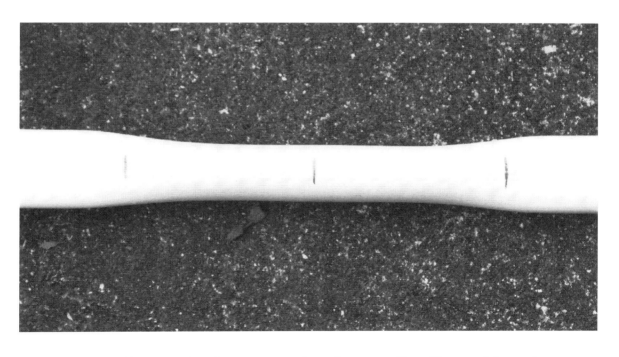

The handle is 6 inches long, centered on the center line. Heat and form the handle starting from an inch outside the handle marks.

Take-Down Archery

With a tile saw or nock file, cut two notches into both ends of the bow. These will be temporary string nocks. They should be centered, 1/2 an inch apart and 1/4 inch deep.

To string up the bow for the first time, hold the bow with the belly facing away from you. Place the bottom loop over the bottom nock and brace the lower limb on your left foot (If you are left-handed, do the opposite). With your right hand, hold the top limb of the bow and hold the top loop in your left. The string you use should be 43 inches long.

Egyptian - Initial Tuning

Step over the bow with your right foot, enough to brace the handle of the bow against the back of your knee. Keep your knee slightly bent. Hold the string taught with your left hand and grip the upper limb firmly below the nock with your right.

With the lower limb braced against your left foot, straighten out your right knee while at the same time pushing the top limb forward. Bring the string loop over to the nock and keep pressing forward until the string slides on to the nock. Before releasing pressure, make sure the string is firmly in both nocks.

Take-Down Archery

Here it is. Because the nocks are cut shallower than they will be, the bow is at a much higher brace than it will be when finished. This is to help bring out any faults early on. If the bow is obviously unbalanced, go back and re-flatten the limbs. If one limb is bending much more than the other, gently heat it up until it gets a little thicker. This should balance the limbs.

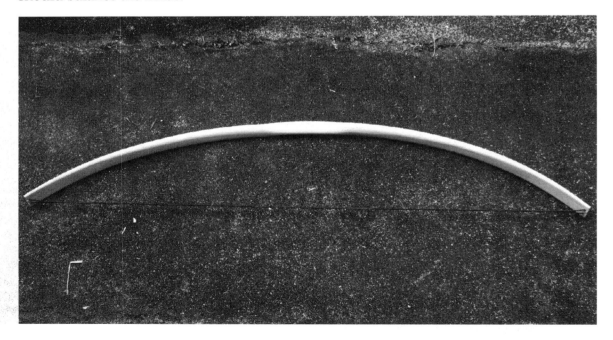

Here's a good example of limb balance. Because the arrow will not rest at exactly the center of the bow, one limb will need to be just a little more flexible than the other. This limb, which is the right limb in the picture will become the top limb and the stiffer limb will become the bottom limb.

Egyptian - Shifting Center

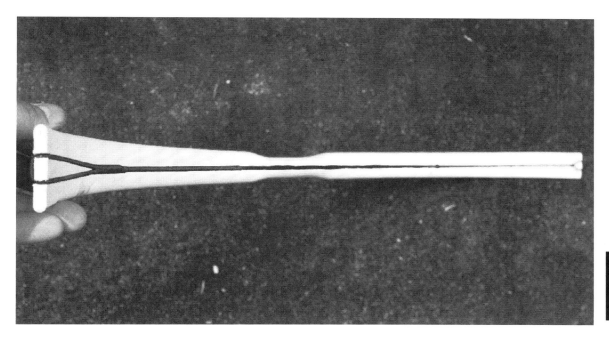

From the end, we can see how the string is centered and runs through the middle of the handle. This bow will put a large deflection in the arrow when the bow is fired. While this can be compensated for, it can be reduced by allowing the arrow to sit closer to center.

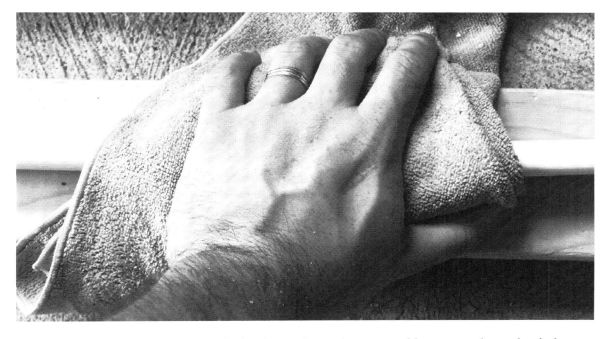

To do this, heat the handle back up along the top and bottom, where the fades are. Once the fades are soft, press the bow handle down. The back of the bow is facing down. If you are right handed, the top limb will be on the left here. If you are left handed, it will be on the right.

Take-Down Archery

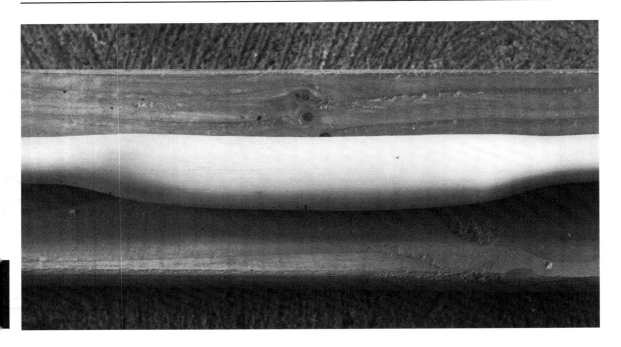

Once the handle has mostly set but is still slightly flexible, make sure both limbs are still balanced and that the handle shaping hasn't twisted the limbs.

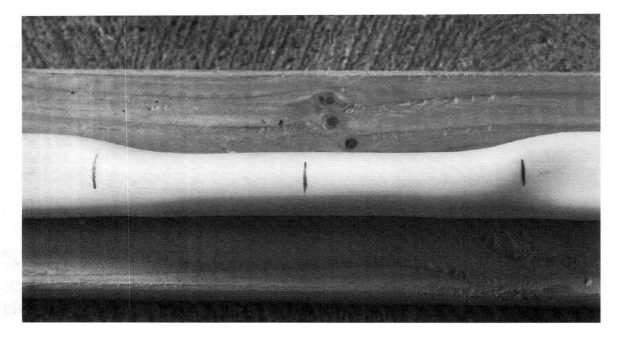

From the back side you can see how the handle is pushed to the side. This will allow an arrow to sit much closer to center without giving the handle a weak spot to collapse sideways.

Egyptian - Shifting Center

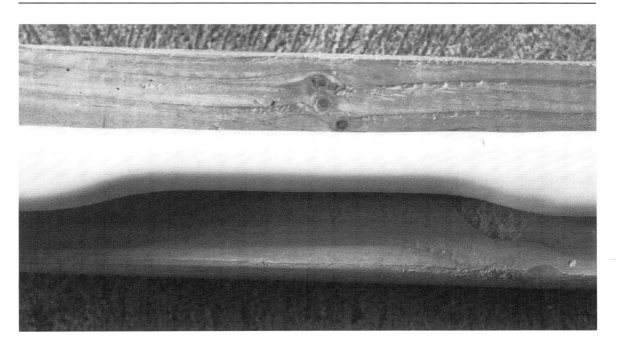

From the belly side, notice how the handle clearance is on the left side of the left limb and the clearance is on the right side of the right limb. Right handed shooters want to put the arrow on the left side of the bow and the opposite is true of left handed shooters.

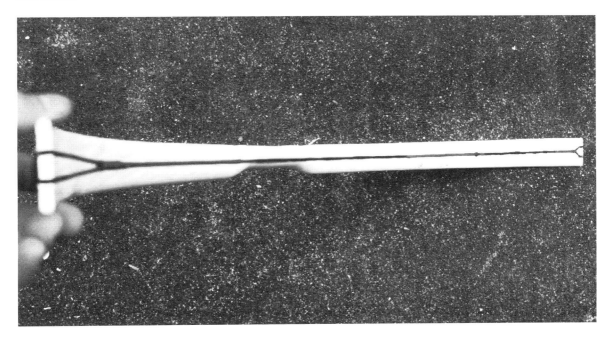

You can see just how closer to center the arrow will pass on this bow. The outside of the handle is almost one continuous line while the inside cuts sharply to give clearance for the arrow.

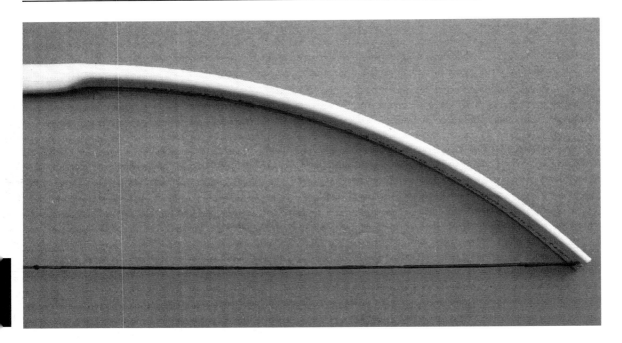

In order to establish the extreme reflex of this style of bow, string the bow backwards with the same string. This will bring the bow to a forced reflex of seven or so inches. While the bow is strung backwards, trace the limb on a background as a template.

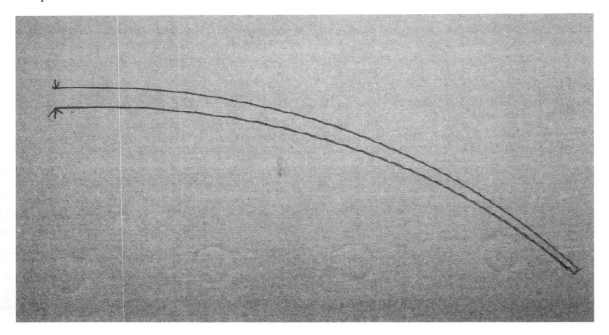

Here's the template. By stringing the bow up backwards we have a perfect opposite bend to our limbs that will result in the characteristic triangular shape of the finished bow.

Egyptian - Reflexing and Deflexing

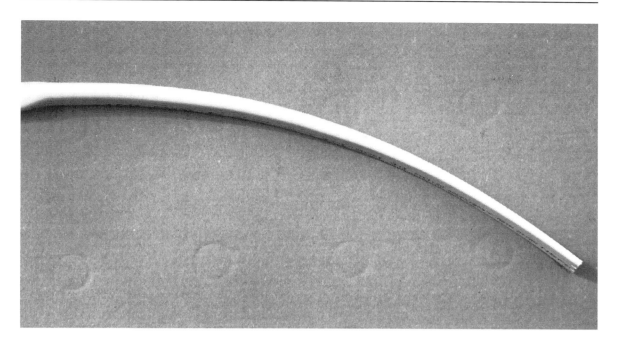

Heat the limb up gently enough to flex it to match the outline. Essentially we want the bow to look like it is strung up backwards without the string.

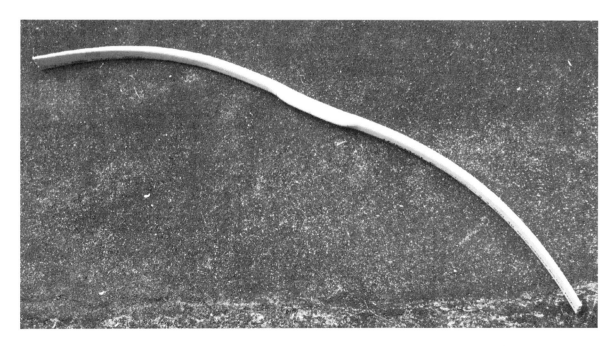

Repeat on the other limb to complete the reflex. Both limbs should be as even as possible to prevent the bow from being unbalanced. A good way to get the flex right is to heat the bow only slightly and then flex it to shape rather than make it lose its shape first, which will leave you with no guide.

Gently heat only the center of the handle in preparation to deflex the handle. Once the handle starts getting soft enough to flex, slowly flex the handle back and forth.

This needs to be done gently of the back of the bow will get stretched out and thinned, creating a weak spot. Just take it slow. If done gently enough, the handle will compress and shift enough to keep the back of the bow strong.

Egyptian - Reflexing and Deflexing

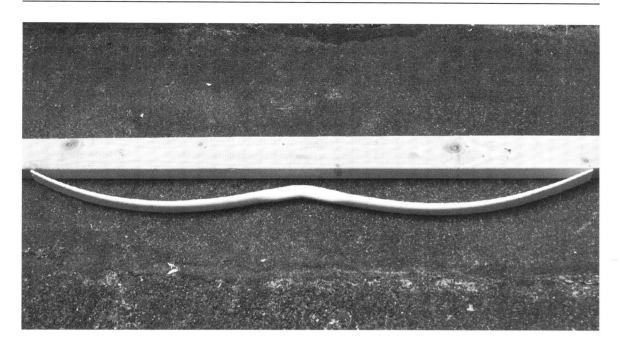

Flex the handle back until the tips of the bow sit about an inch in front of the handle when placed against a flat surface. Any small variations in limb flex can be adjusted by flexing the handle slightly toward the less reflexed limb.

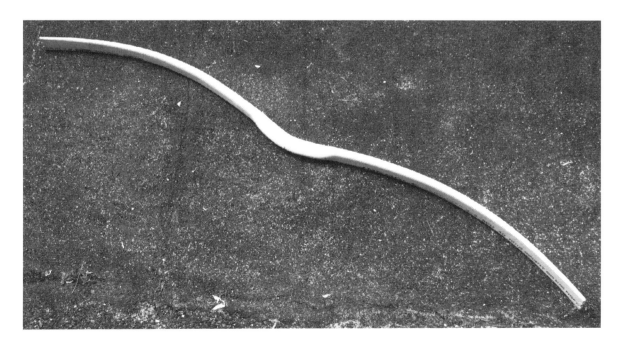

With the handle deflexed and the limbs reflexed, we are now ready to build the siyahs or ears of the bow's limbs where the string will be attached.

Take-Down Archery

Start with two lengths of 1/2 inch schedule 40 pipe, 6 inches long. These will become the tips of the bow and will hold the string.

Using the 3/4 inch spacer blocks, flatten both pipes with a taper. Place the pipe right at the beginning of the spacer block and use the very end of the flattening board so that the very end is flattened shut.

Egyptian - Making and Attaching Siyahs

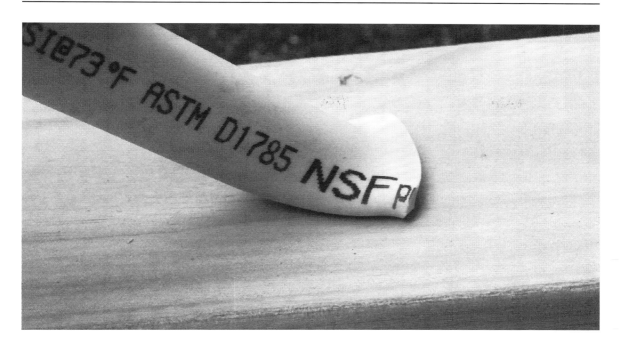

Heat up the open end of the pipe and press it down at a 35-40 degree angle. This will establish the angle the siyahs go into the bow. Make sure both siyahs match.

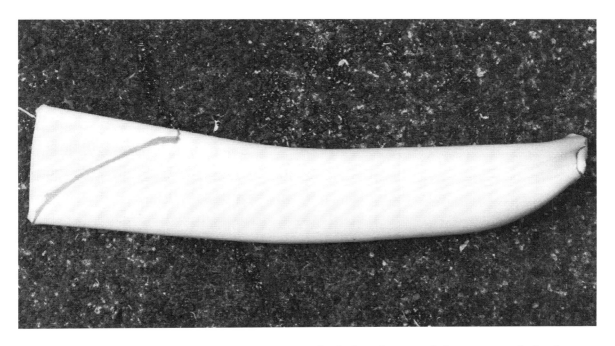

Heat the siyah up gently and give it a slight bend toward the non-angled edge, which will be on the back side of the bow. The two inches of this siyah will be above the nock, so there's room for a little creativity. Draw the shape you want for the nock, here I have a simple curve.

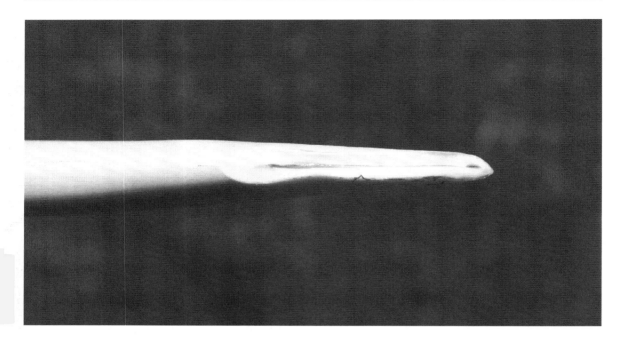

Follow the line and cut the excess off. Then heat the very end of the pipe and flatten it so that there are no gaps. A little bit of glue before closing the end off helps completely seal the siyah.

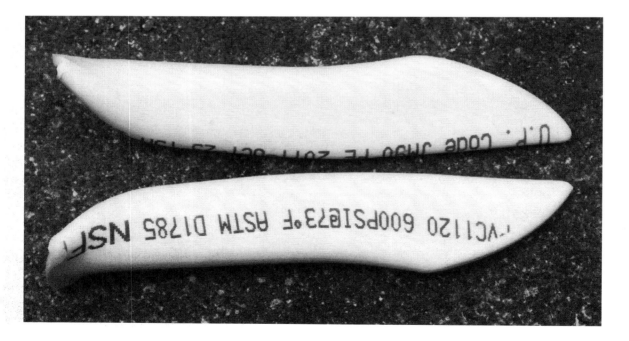

Finish off the end of the siyah with some sandpaper and round off any sharp edges in preparation to attach the siyahs to the bow.

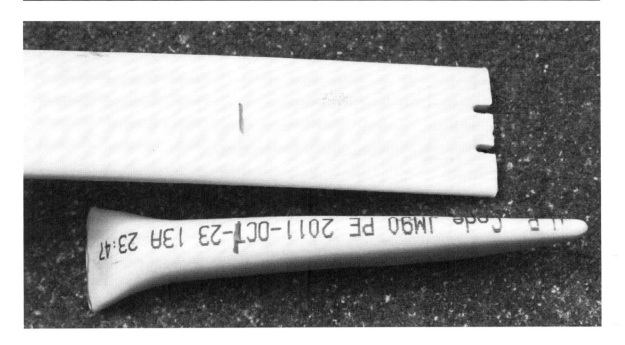

Mark 2 inches from the bottom of the siyah and 3 inches from the end of your bow. These will mark where the two will overlap, and the 3 inches from the bow will be cut off.

Cut the 3 bow at the 3 inch mark and then round off the edges so that the bow blends well with the siyahs.

Take-Down Archery

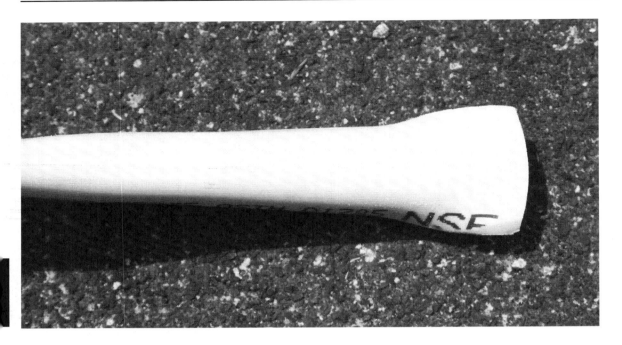

File or sand down the base of the siyah so that there is enough of a taper to grip the inside of the bow but not enough to deform its shape. By knocking off the corners the transition will be much smoother.

Gently heat 2 inches of the end of the pipe until it puff up to its original cylindrical shape. Once it's soft enough, insert the siyahs until it goes in to the two inch mark. A little bit of epoxy or other adhesive can be added to reinforce the joint.

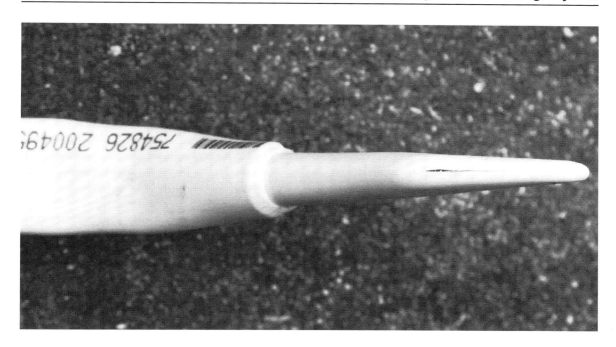

While the joint is still soft, make sure the siyah sits straight in the bow and lines up with the other nock.

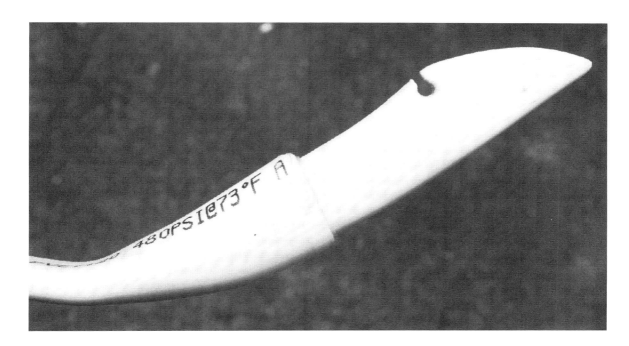

Measure 2 inches down from the end and cut your nock with a nock file or tile saw. The nock should be 1/4 inch deep and a little more than 1/8 inch wide. Making the nock round like this will prevent the string from slipping out when the bow is drawn.

Take-Down Archery

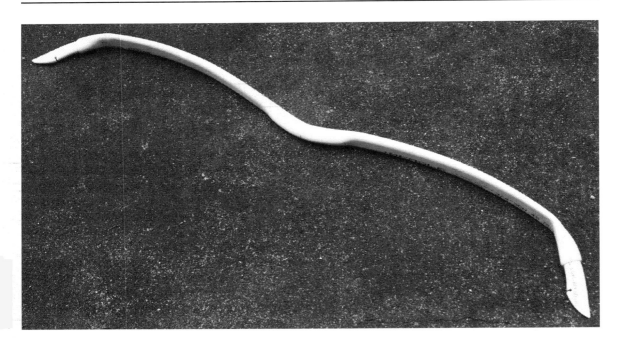

Repeat on the other limb. Make sure to keep the angle on both limbs equal. Having an even angle on the base of your siyahs should keep things balanced.

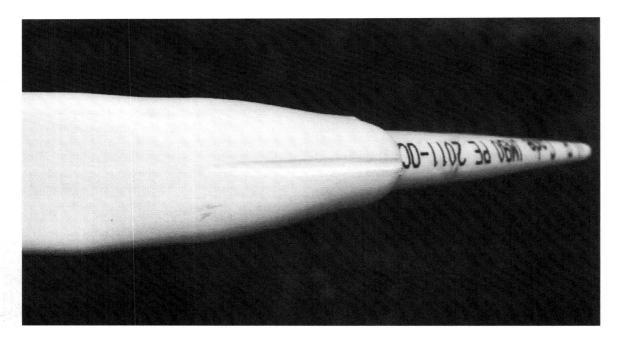

To help the string track down the two recurves, file a groove at least 1/8 inch wide around the belly side of the joint between siyah and limb.

Egyptian - Fine Tuning

When braced, the bow resembles a very flat and wide triangle. The bow should be gripped with the web between thumb and index finger resting on the inside of the handle bend.

Here the bow is drawn to 28 inches. At this length it reaches 35 pounds. One of the advantages to this bow's shape is that it can be drawn further, about 45 pounds at 30 inches.

Take-Down Archery

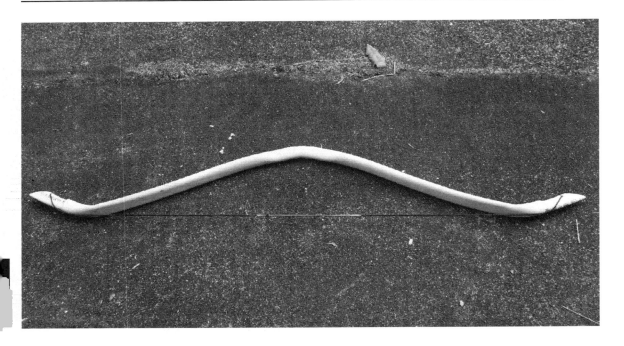

This is a good amount of limb balance for this bow. Notice that one siyah has a slightly greater angle to compensate for a weak limb.

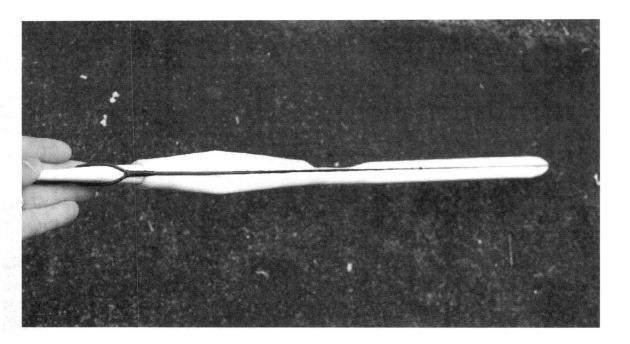

Make sure that the bow's siyahs line up along the limbs when the bow is strung or it might twist and unstring itself when drawn and shot. Here you can see the off-center handle which allows for more forgiveness in the shot.

Egyptian - Three Piece Take Down

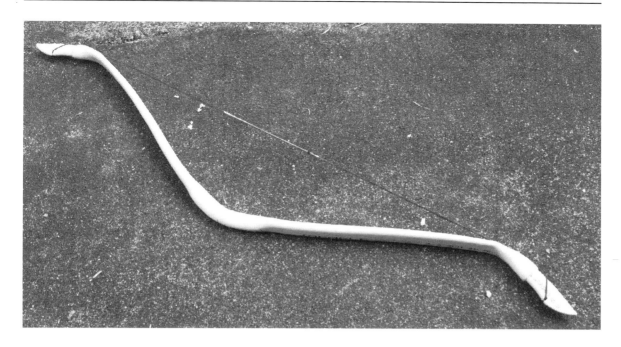

Here's the completed bow, ready to shoot. Make sure any issues with shape and alignment are done now as it will be difficult once the bow is in multiple pieces.

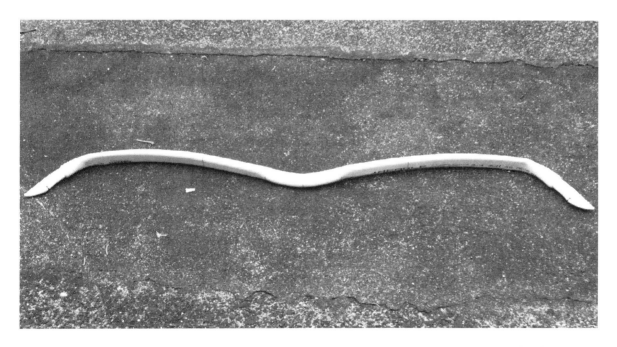

To figure out where to cut the bow for a 3 piece take down, measure the bow from tip to tip, straight across rather than along the limbs. Take that length, minus 2 inches and then divide by 3. The two end pieces will be that length and the middle section will be that length plus 2 inches.

Take-Down Archery

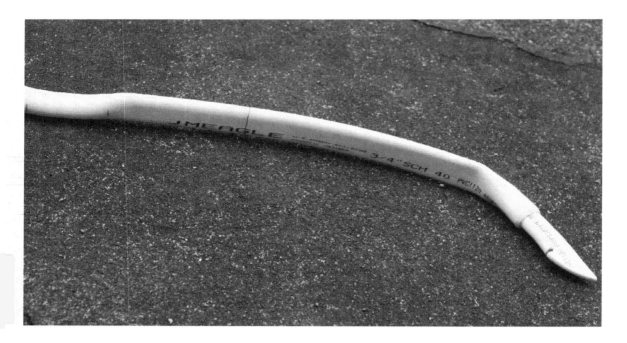

The formula for this is **piece length = (length of bow - 2) / 3**. Once you have that, add 2 inches for the center piece. For example, a 44 inch from tip to tip bow will result in two 14 inch limb pieces and a 16 inch handle section.

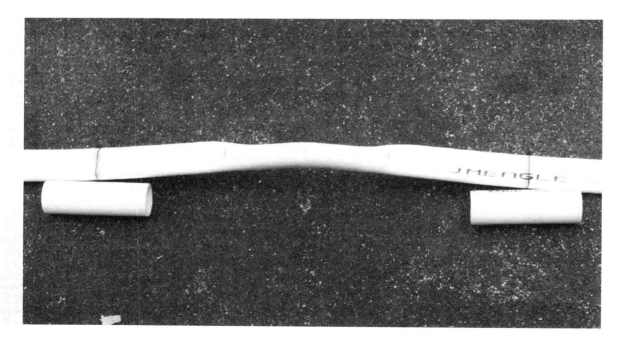

Take two 4 inch lengths of 1 inch schedule 40 pipe and sand down the sharp edges. These will become the connectors once the bow is cut.

Egyptian - Three Piece Take Down

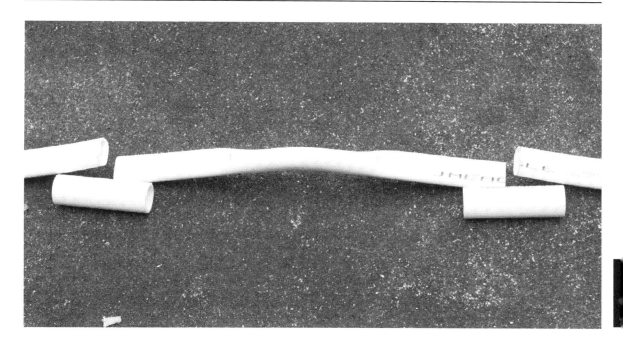

Cut the bow into three pieces on the lines you marked. This should be a clean cut. While a saw would work, a PVC pipe cutter works best for this because it does not remove any material.

It's alright for the cut to have a slight angle to it, as this will help the two sides fit together better and reduce any possibility of the connectors slipping, Sand the outside edges just slightly to remove any burs and allows the parts to fit better later.

Take-Down Archery

Heat up one of the connectors until it is completely soft. 1 inch pipe, once soft, will slide over 3/4 inch pipe. Just like flattening a bow limb, the connector should completely yield to finger pressure before it's soft enough.

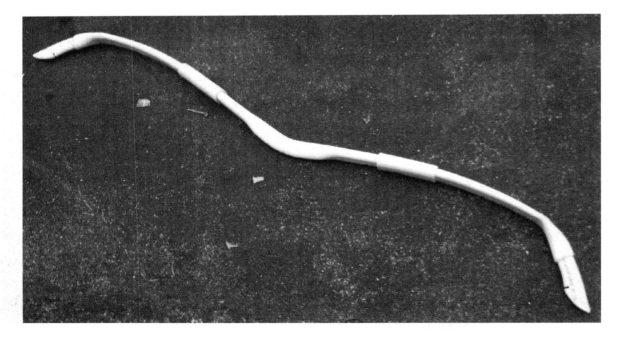

Reconnect the pieces of the pipe by sliding the bow pieces into the flexible connectors while they are still hot. Once the connector sets, it can be removed. Place a little glue onto the outer limb sections to permanently bond the limb to the connector.

Egyptian - Finishing

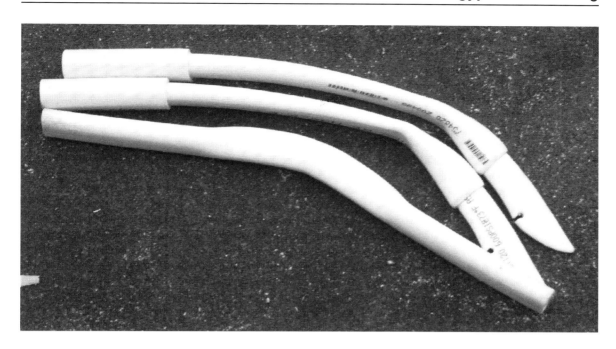

When broken down, the bow takes up little space, and the curved section compliment each other. To ensure smooth shooting and ease of break-down, some form of lubricant can be applied to the inside of the connectors. Other than that, enjoy your new bow!

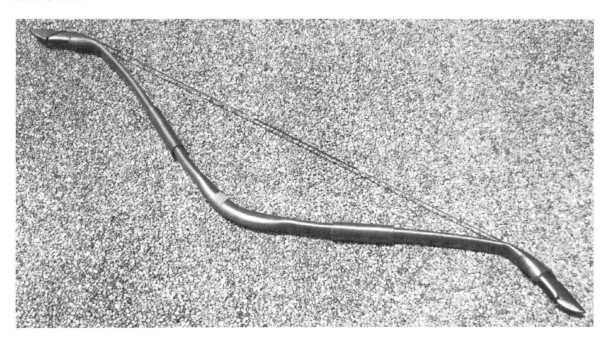

Here's the finished bow. This bow was finished with a specialty plastic spray paint. When painting a bow, make sure to paint it while the connectors are in place. Otherwise, the thin layer of paint will keep the connector from fitting and coming off easily.

Take-Down Archery

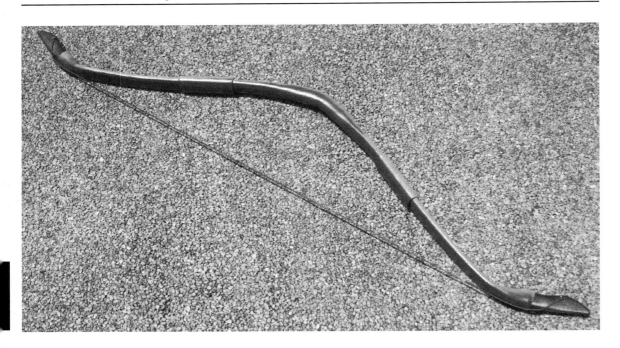

This bow was painted black and then the back side was painted orange. The tips were painted with a silver overspray after wrapping the limbs with masking tape. When selecting paint, look for UV resistance. Some paints need a UV-resistant clear coat over them to ensure longevity.

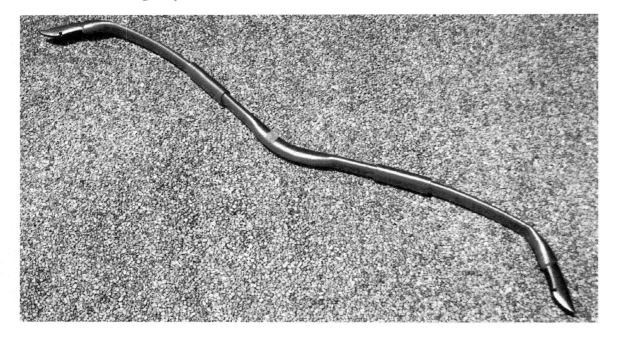

Once the bow has been used for a while and settles into its final set, it should look something like this. The recurves and reflex will help keep the bow at very low string follow.

Chapter Five
Tracker

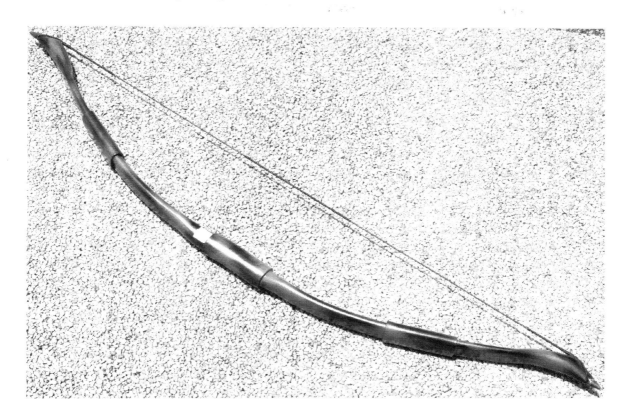

     This bow is ideal when space is limited. The name tracker fits this compact and powerful bow, a bow based loosely on the short bows of America's West Coast. It's small, and without any recurves it breaks down into straight pieces that pack easily. While it lacks the benefit of recurves or a large reflex, it makes up for it with a good deal of power and quiet shooting. It is very quiet to shoot.

     This bow works very well broken down into two pieces and is very compact. For a little extra space, the bow can be broken down to four pieces and still perform. It's a great little bow that can be stored just about anywhere and because it's made of PVC, it can be stored in and around water without any issues.

     It's not the most forgiving bow to shoot and at this bow to draw length combination is very rough on the fingers. This bow is a good candidate for using a release as both accuracy and speed improve. Since it's such a stressed bow, I wouldn't use this as an everyday shooter, though it would work well for that if needed.

     This bow is ideal as a backup or a bow that can be left in the bottom of a bag or pack and forgotten. At least until it is needed.

Take-Down Archery

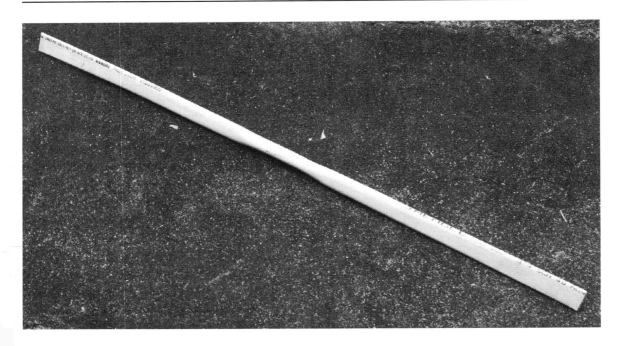

Taper flatten a 46 inch long, 3/4 inch schedule 40 pipe. Use the 3/4 inch spacer block and start at 3 inches from the center.

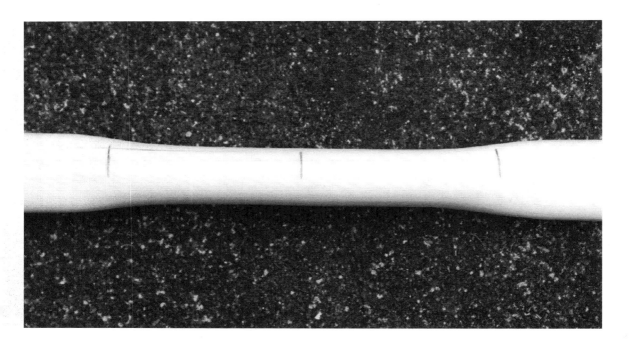

Starting at 3 inches from center will result in a 6 inch handle. Heat and form the handle like the reflex/deflex bow, forming the handle to be a little taller than it is wide.

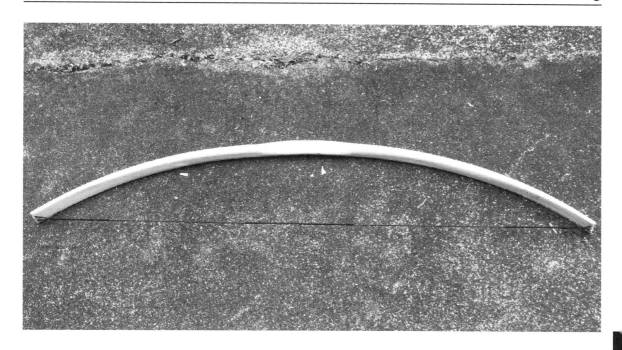

Cut temporary nocks into the ends of the bow and string it to brace with a 40 inch string. Find the limb that is bending more, it will become the upper limb. In this case it's the left limb.

Mark 1/2 an inch from the end of the bow and 5 inches from the 1/2 inch mark. This will be formed into non-bending limb tips.

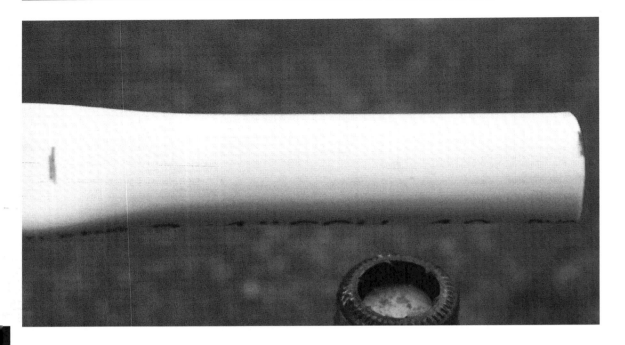

Cut off the 1/2 inch end section and heat the end up until the pipe returns to its normal shape.

While it is still soft enough to form, press the base down so that the back of the bow is flush with the back side of the new siyah. At the same time, lift the end of the siyah up until the bottom of the siyah lines up with the main limb.

Tracker - Shaping Nocks and Handle

Once the siyah has set, re-heat the belly side and end of the siyah. With a bench vise or the ends of your fattening jig, smash the end of the siyah at an angle to close up the end.

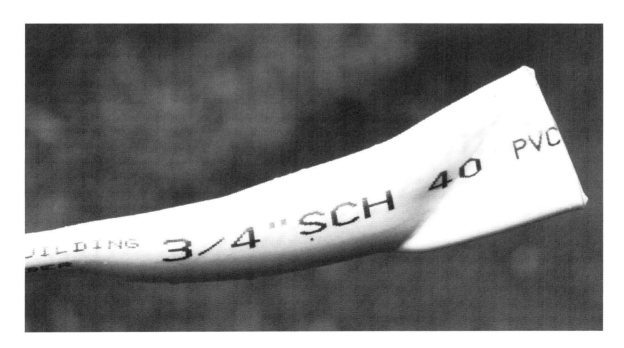

This is what the tip should look like. You can vary the angle of the end, but this angle will allow most commercial string loops to fit over the nocks. If making your own, feel free to shape this however you like.

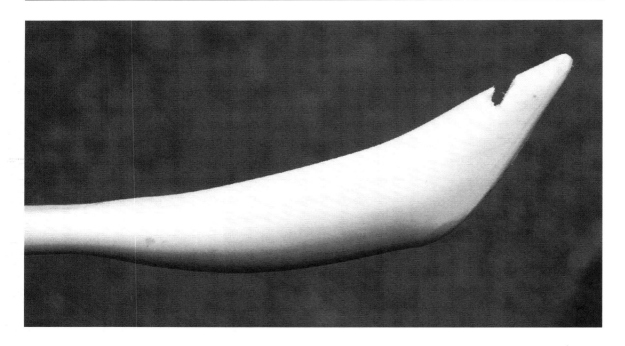

Cut the flattened tab away and sand the back edge of the bow tip. With a tile saw or nock file, cut a 1/4 inch keep groove at an angle to hold the string.

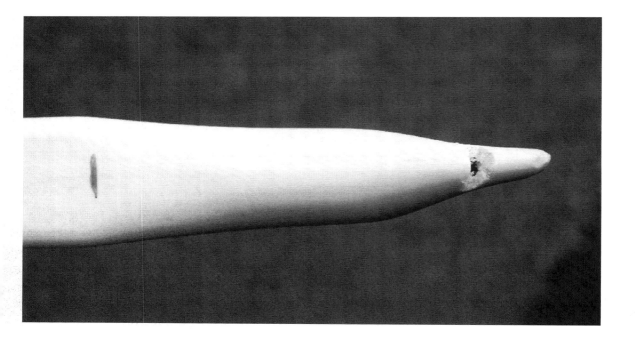

Here is another view of the bow tip from the top, or back of the bow.

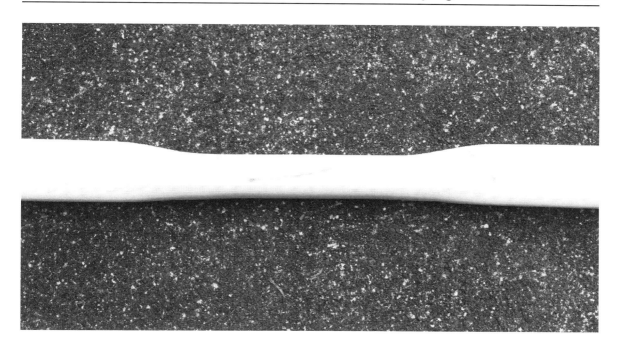

Go back to the handle and heat it up just enough to push the handle to the side to bring the arrow closer to center.

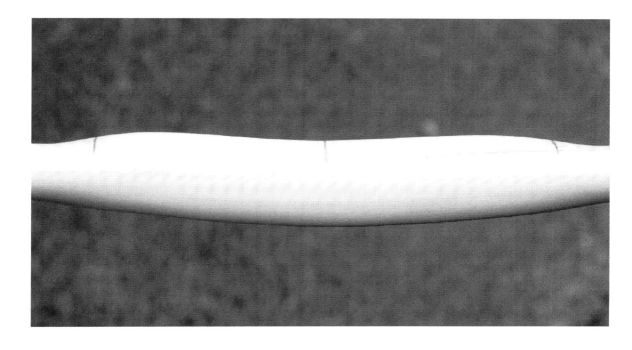

While the handle is still slightly soft, flex it toward the back of the bow slightly to give the bow some reflex in the handle.

Take-Down Archery

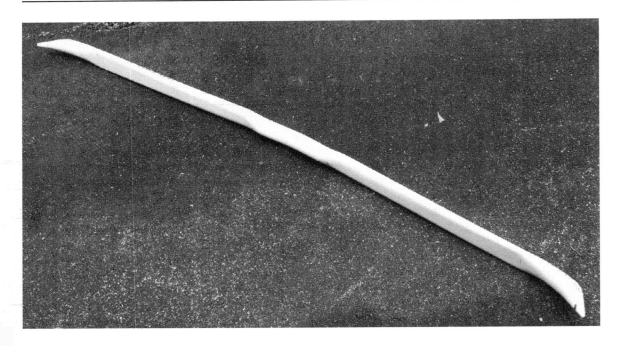

Here is the bow, ready to be strung up.

Here is the bow braced. The top limb bends just a little more than the lower limb. Grip the bow around the center of the handle, the top of your hand resting about 2 inches from center.

Tracker - Fine Tuning

Here the bow is drawn to 28 inches. At this length it reaches 40 pounds. It's a very short bow, though it still can be drawn to a full 28 inches, it's maximum draw length.

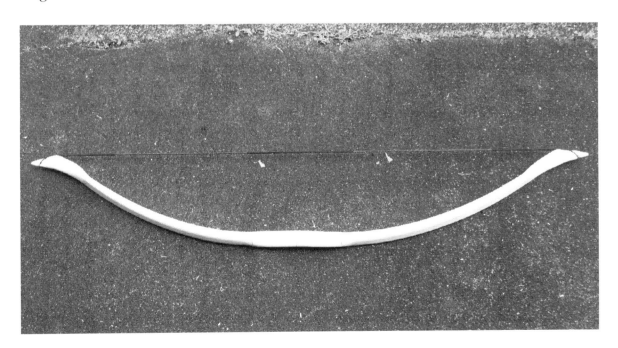

Here's the bow at brace. The left limb is the top limb of the bow. If the limbs are slightly out of alignment, a gentle pull on the stronger limb alone may help even things out. If this does not work, gently heat the weaker limb until it thickens slightly.

Take-Down Archery

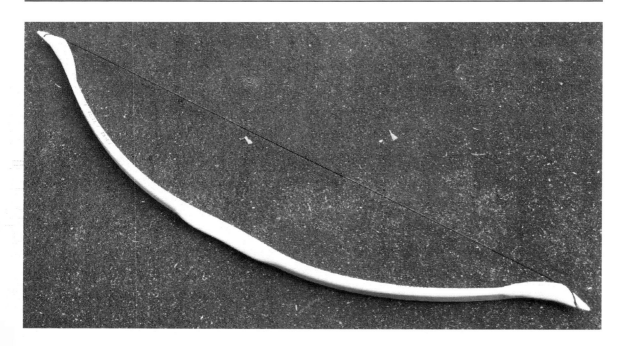

The bow is now ready to be used, as is. Before applying any finish or continuing to make the bow a take-down, make sure to break the bow in. Fix any problems that may arise before cutting the bow apart, as any fixes will be difficult later.

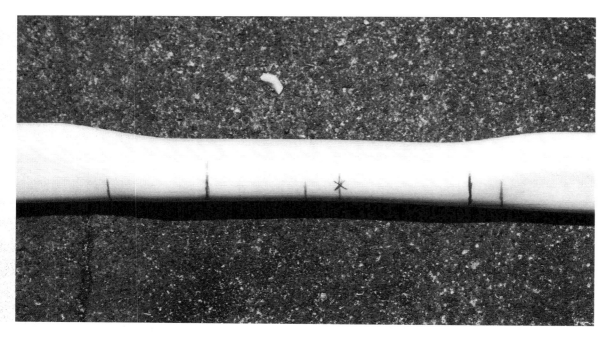

Mark the new handle where the connector sleeve will go. The shorter marks are the old handle marks. The center, which will be the cut line, is marked with an x. It is located 1/2 and inch away from the old center. Mark 2 inches from the new center, forming a 4 inch handle.

Tracker - Two Piece Take Down

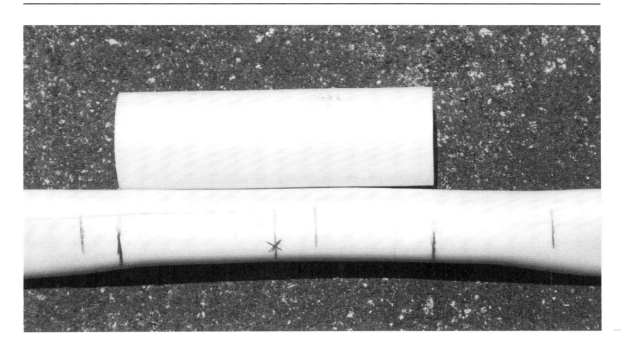

Cut a length of 1 inch, schedule 40 PVC pipe, 4 inches long. The center will line up with the cut line and become the connector.

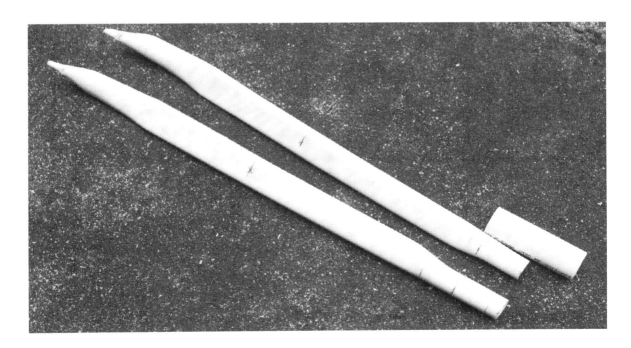

Cut the bow in half along the cut line. The lower limb should be shorter than the top limb to the point where the extra 2 inches bring them close to each other in length.

Take-Down Archery

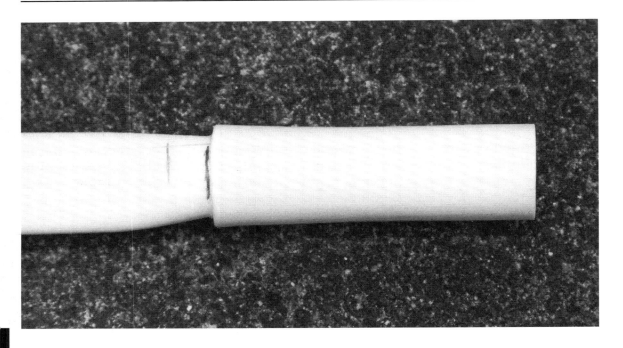

Heat up the handle connector and glue it into place over the lower limb, going down to the 2 inch mark.

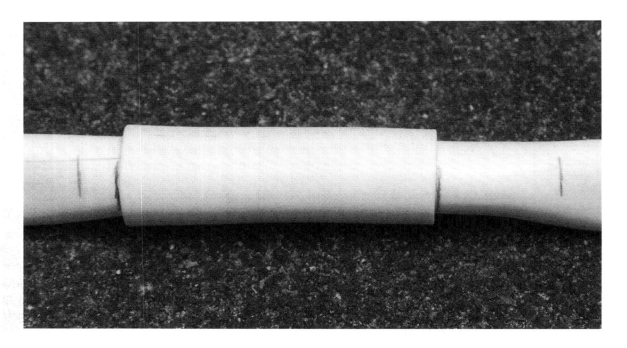

While the handle piece is still hot, press the top limb in place. To help facilitate easier removal later, coat the 2 inch handle section of the top limb with a wax or dry lubricant.

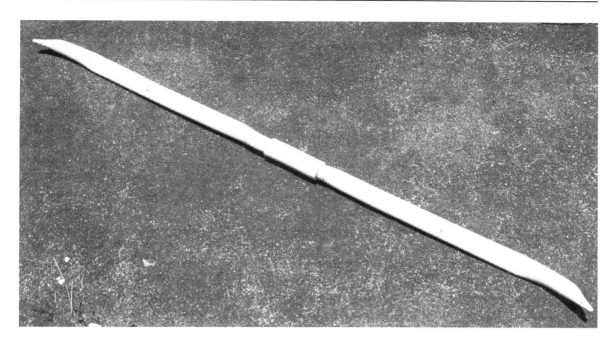

With the handle in place and before it fully cools, sight down the bow and make sure the tips and limbs line up. The handle should be very snug should not rotate or wiggle at this point.

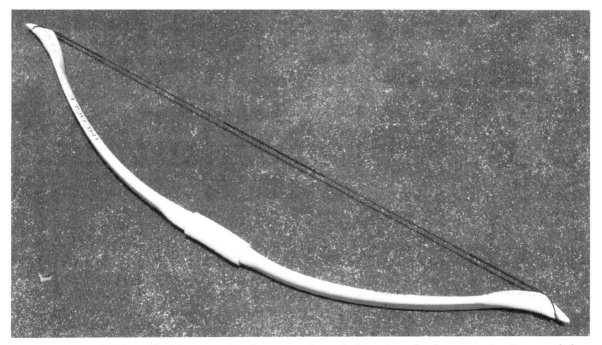

Once the handle his completely set and cooled, string the bow again. Be careful when stringing the bow as a poorly-fitting handle may slip out when being strung. Once strung, give the bow a few short draws to warm it up. There should be no creaking and the handle should not be slipping. It is a good idea to wear eye protection when breaking the bow in as a poor fit may cause the bow to pull apart at full draw.

Take-Down Archery

To find where your limb cuts will be for a 4-piece bow, use this formula: **piece length = (length of bow - 4) / 4**. Add 2 inches tot he two center sections. So if your bow is 44 inches long from tip to tip, your end pieces will be 10 inches long each and your handle pieces will be 12 inch long each. Keep in mind that you should already have center cut by now, so this formula only applies to the outer limbs.

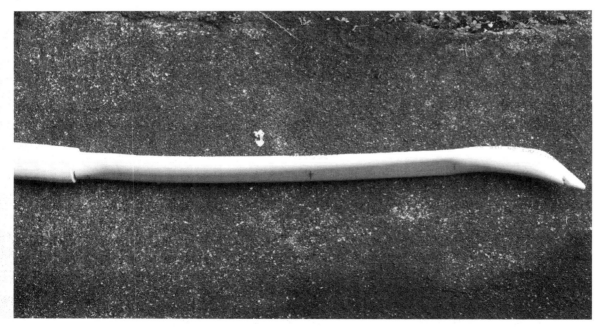

Here's a close-up of where the limb will be cut. Make sure your measurements are correct, as it is very easy to make your limb pieces uneven by cutting in the wrong spot. If your limb pieces are uneven your could end up with a non-working bow.

Tracker - Four Piece Take Down

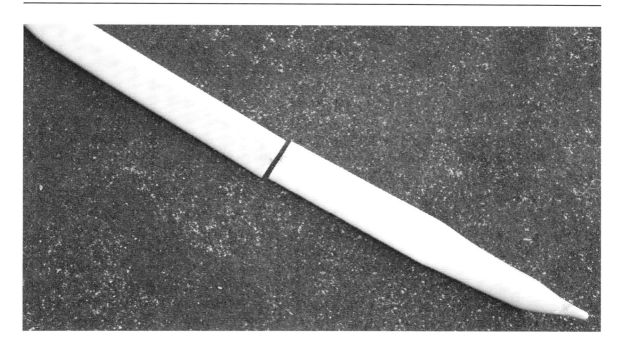

Cut along the limb cut mark. This can be made slightly angled to help keep the limbs from twisting. This should be very slight, as too much of an angle can cause the connector to set up crooked.

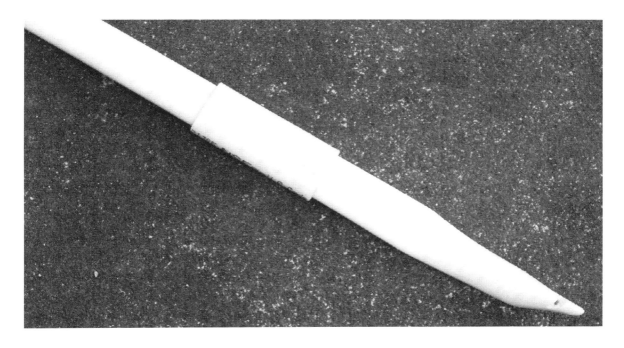

Heat up a 4 inch connector made from 1 inch schedule 40 PVC pipe. The side on the limb's tip should be glued on to the limb. The other side should be able to come out of the connector.

Take-Down Archery

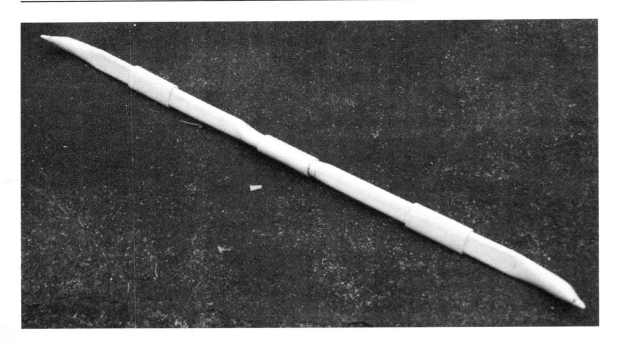

With the connectors still warm, sight down the bow and make sure the limbs line up as they did before. As with the 2 and 3 piece take-down bows, make sure to take great caution when stringing and shooting the bow. Take it slow and wear eye protection until the bow is broken in.

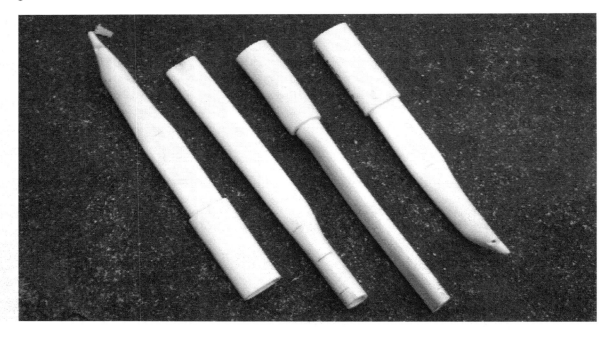

Broken down, this is one of the most compact bows that can be made, with each piece only a little over a foot long.

Tracker - Finishing

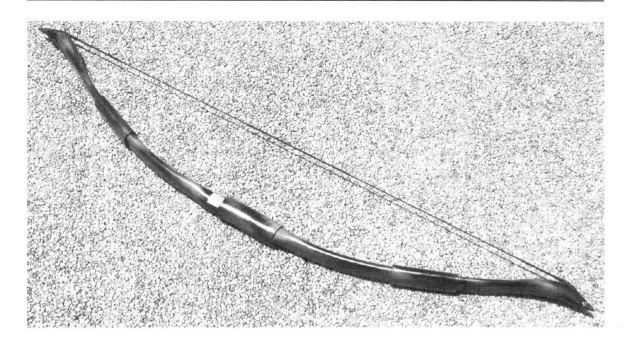

This bow was finished with a simple spray of paint. It's a simple camouflage with gray primer, a khaki brown, hunter green and black.

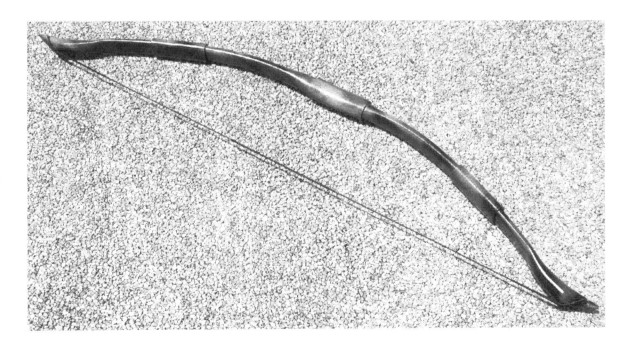

An alternate view of the bow from the belly side. Make sure to paint the bow assembled as the paint may prevent the internal connector pieces from fitting together if paint gets on them.

Take-Down Archery

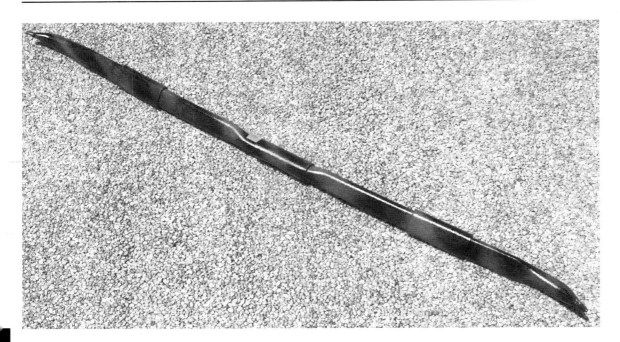

The bow from the back, unstrung. The 2 and 4 piece take-down designs work well on 3/4 inch bows. 1 inch bows pose a bit of a challenge and should only be attempted by the advanced PVC bowyer. In the next chapter, we'll tackle a 3 piece takedown made with 1 inch pipe.

Chapter Six
Nomad

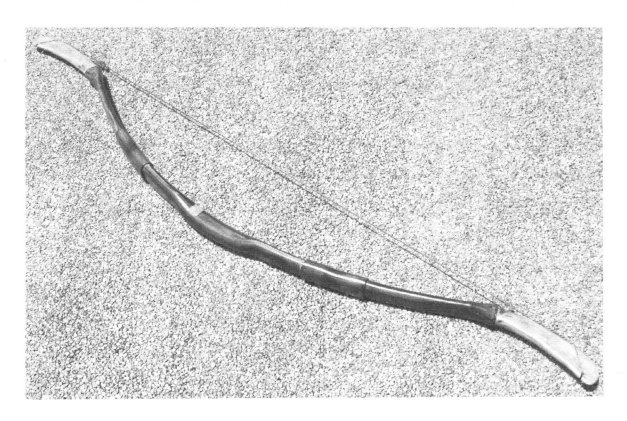

We will go over how to construct an almost recurved bow in a shape reminiscent of Asiatic style composite bows used by the nomads of the Eurasian Steppe. It's a smooth drawing bow with good power and speed. While a little on the long side, once broken down it is small enough to fit into most backpacks and duffel bags.

Unlike bows made from 3/4 and 1/2 inch pipe, bows made from 1 inch pipe do not have an easy source for take down connectors. This is because the next size up, 1 and 1/4 inch pipe has an inner diameter just a little bigger than the outside diameter of 1 inch pipe. In this case, connectors can be made from 1 inch pipe.

This bow, which pulls 45 pound at 28 inches, is made from 1 inch schedule 40 PVC pipe with connectors made from the same. Because 1 inch connectors on a 1 inch bow are not as stiff as if the connector were of a larger diameter, the take-down must be done near midlimb where they can flex freely. Alternatively if you use schedule 80, 1 and 1/4 inch PVC pipe for the connectors, a 1 inch pipe bow can be made in 2, 3 and 4 pieces.

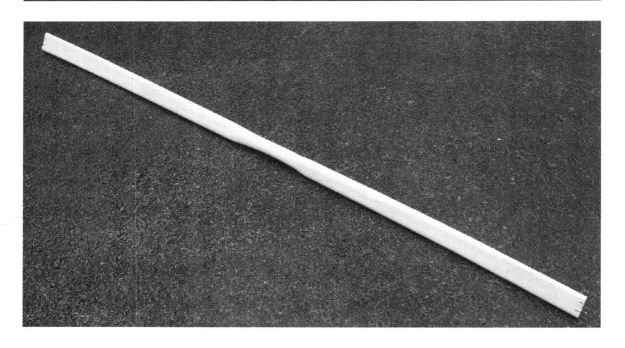

Taper flatten a 1 inch, schedule 40 PVC pipe cut 58 inches long using 1 inch spacers. Start the flattening 3 inches from the center, making a 6 inch handle.

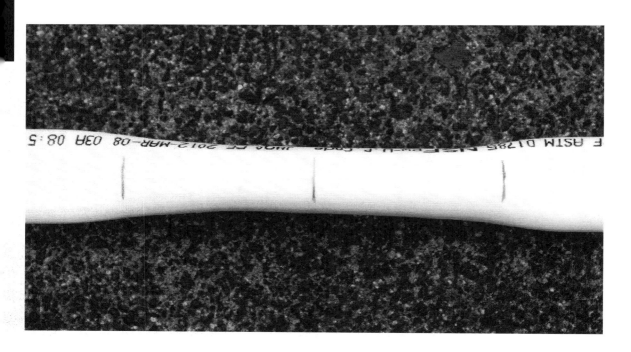

Heat and form the handle. It should be around 1 inch wide.

Nomad - Initial Tuning

Cut temporary nocks into the ends of the bow and mark 8 inches in from each end.

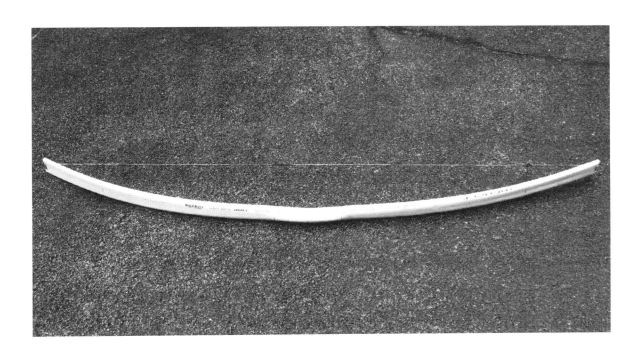

String the bow up with a 53 inch string. The limb that flexes more will become the top limb. On this bow it is the left limb.

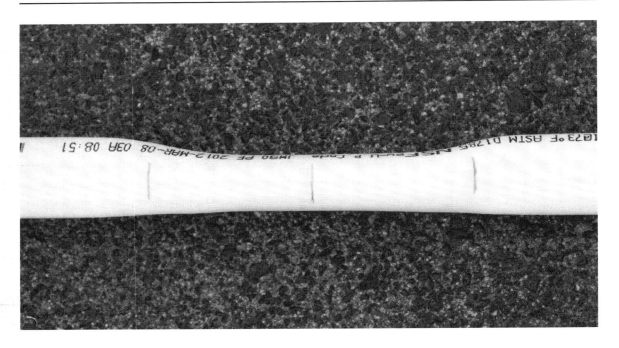

Heat the handle near the fades and press the handle to the side. Make sure that the handle is pushed away from where the arrow will go. For a right handed shooter, the upper limb is to the left and for left handed shooters the upper limb is to the right.

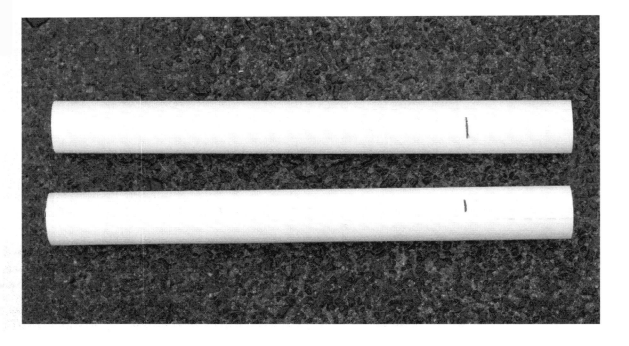

For the siyahs, cut two 10 inch lengths of 3/4 inch schedule 40 pipe. Mark 2 inches from one end of each pipe.

Nomad - Making and Attaching Siyahs

Flatten the pipe to a taper using the 1 inch spacer block and the back end of the flattening jig. This will produce an even taper from the base of the siyah to the tip.

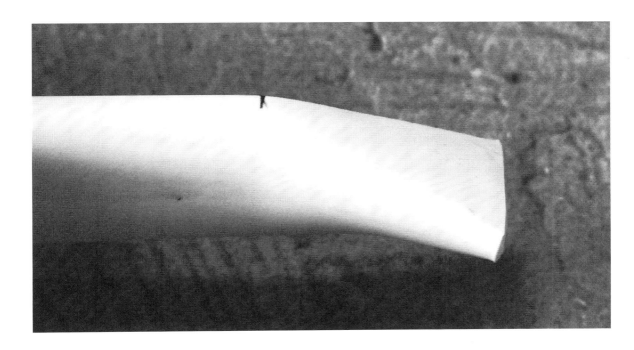

Heat up the last 2 inches of the base and flatten it to a taper.

Take-Down Archery

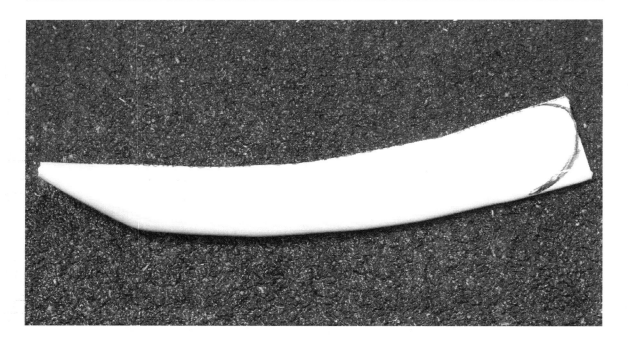

Heat the siyah up carefully and put some reflex into it. Now is a good time to draw the shape of the siyah tip.

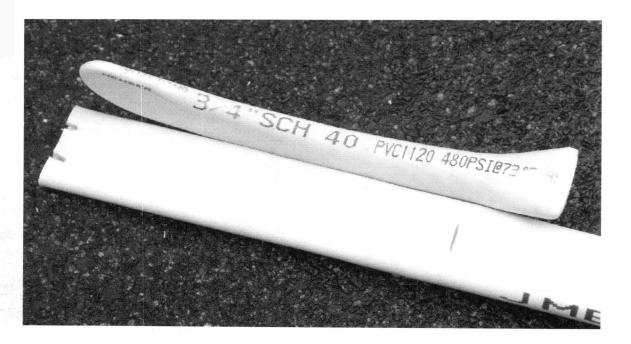

Cut along the lines and sand the siyah down. Notice that the base of the siyah is ground down so that it will blend smoothly with the limb and not deform the edges. Here it is, next to the bow limb. This is where it will sit once the extra end is cut away.

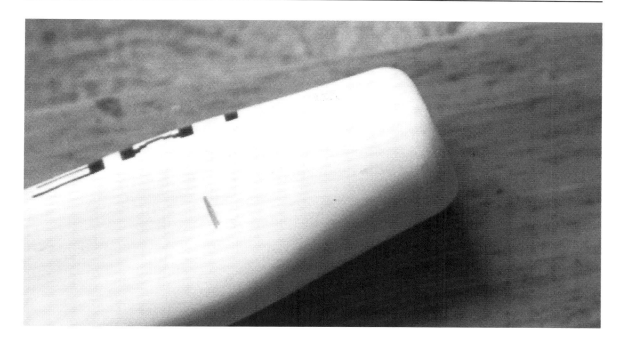

Cut off at the 8 inch mark and then make a new mark 2 inches down from the end. Heat the end of the pipe up until it returns to round. Grind the edges down for a smooth transition.

Heat the end of the limb until it is soft again and press the siyahs into it for 2 inches. An adhesive will help the siyah bond with the limb and will prevent any creaking or noise. Cut a 1/2 an inch groove 3/4 inches away from the end of the tip to form the string nock.

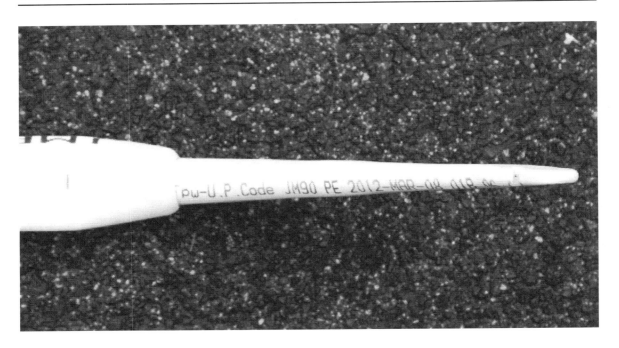

Here's an alternate view of the siyah to limb connection from the top. Make sure to sight down the limbs from tip to tip to make sure they line up.

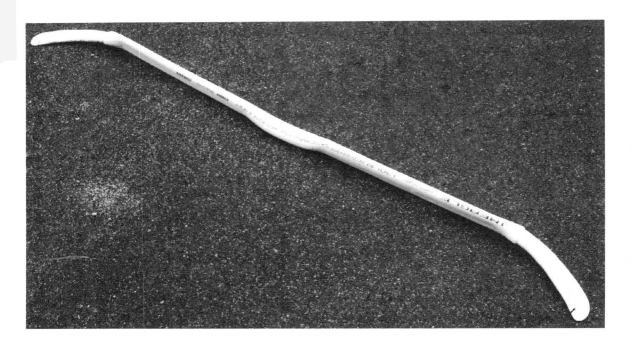

The bow is now ready to be strung for the first time.

Nomad - Fine Tuning

Strung, the reflexed tips should be reflexed only enough for the string to come close to touching the siyahs. The string shouldn't rest on the siyahs themselves aside from the top where the loops are.

At a full 28 inch draw this bow pulls 45 pounds. This bow will pull to 32 inches. If made with takedown connectors, a bow of these dimensions should not exceed 28 inches of draw.

Take-Down Archery

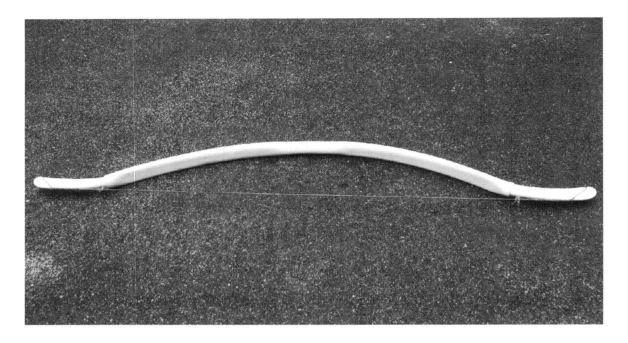

At brace, the top limb should be flexing just a little more than the other limb. In this case, the left limb, which is the top limb, is flexing more. This is about the most imbalance acceptable for a bow of this length.

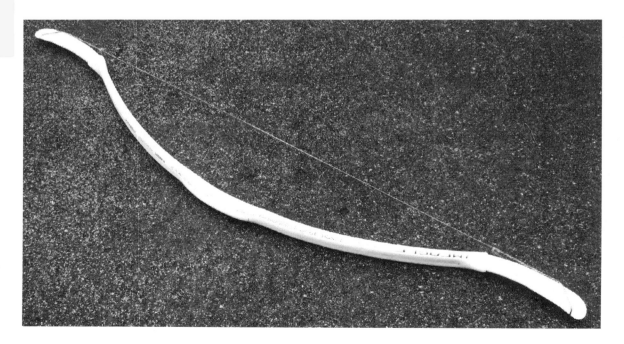

The bow is finished and ready to be shot out. Make sure that you break the bow in before final finishing to breaking the bow down.

Nomad - Three Piece Take Down

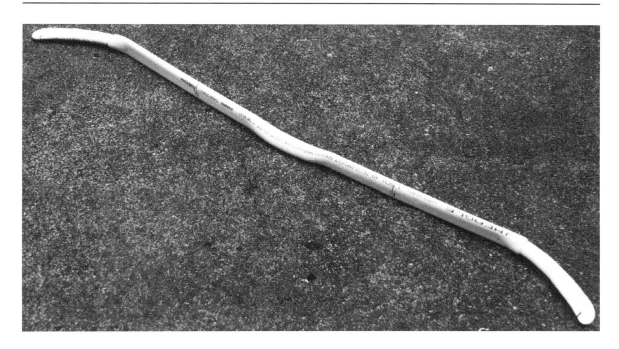

To find where to make the limb cuts, use the same formula as the Desert Viper. The formula for this is **piece length = (length of bow - 2) / 3**. So for this 56 inch long bow, the outer limbs will be 18 inches long and the handle will be 20. When the connectors are added, all sections will be equal.

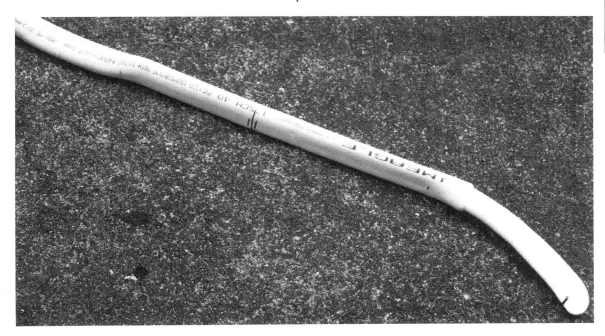

Here's a closeup of one of the limb cuts. It's easier to work around the awkward shape of the bow by measuring both from the end of the limb and the handle. The center mark is the middle point of both marks. This is one way to get more evenly proportioned pieces.

Take-Down Archery

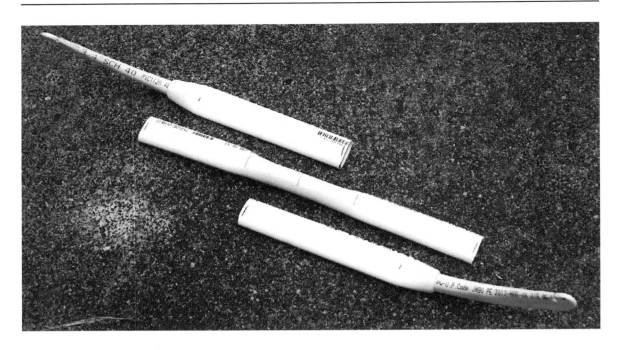

Follow the cut lines and cut the bow into three pieces. The limbs should be 2 inches shorter than the handle.

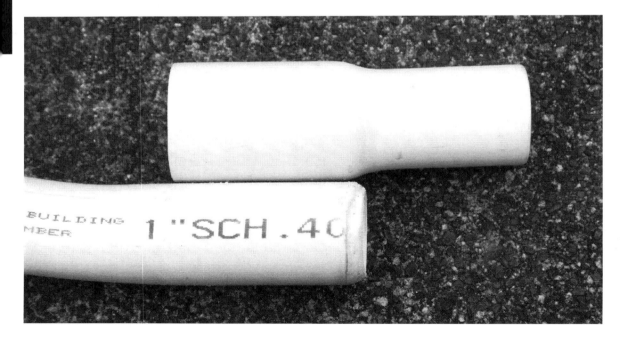

In order to make a 1 inch sleeve fit over 1 inch pipe, it needs to be pre-stretched. This can be done with a scrap piece of 1 inch pipe. Cut your 1 inch, schedule 40 connectors 4 and 1/2 inches long as the connector will shrink a little. 1 inch pipe also requires longer connectors.

Nomad - Three Piece Take Down

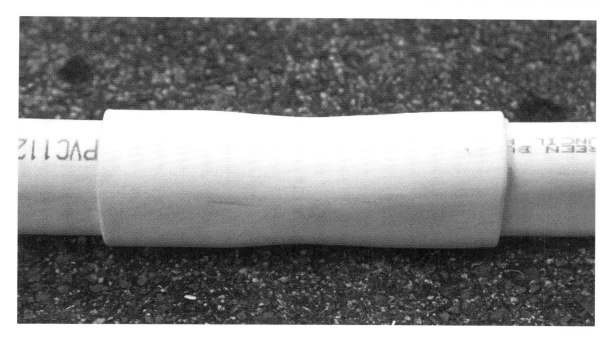

Once pre-stretched, heat the connector and drive the two cut ends together. Glue the outer limb nearest to the end of the bow into the connector. When working with 1 inch pipe, the center of the connector will usually get constricted as the inside pipe gets compressed to a smaller size. As long as the connection is snug and not loose, this should not cause too much weakness.

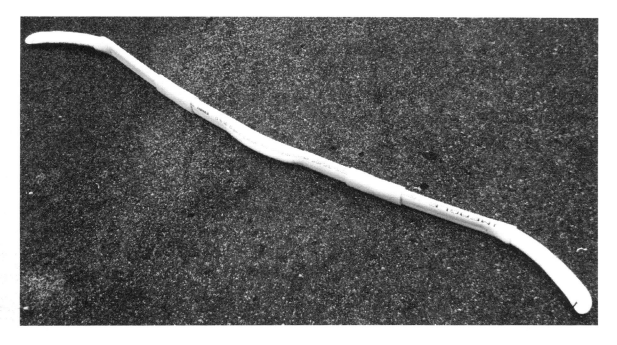

While the connectors are still warm, sight down the bow and make sure everything lines up.

Take-Down Archery

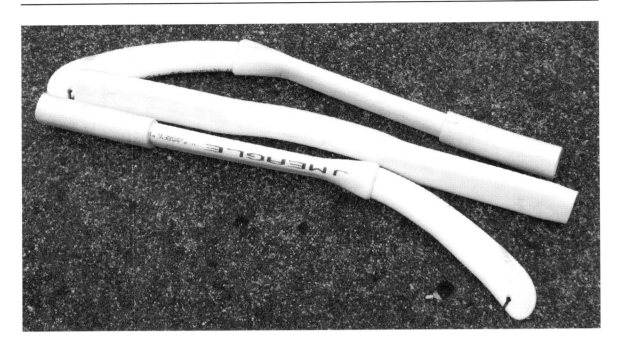

A view of the bow broken down. Notice how the ends of the handle section are actually tapered down from the compressing effect of the 1 inch connector sleeves.

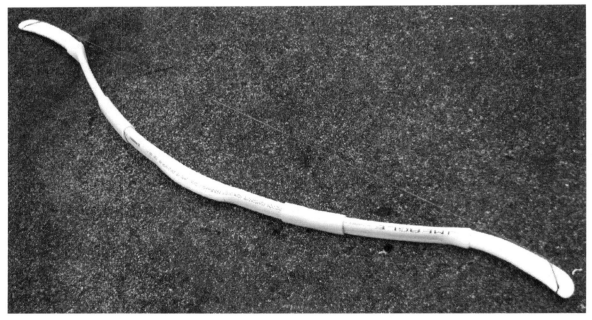

Be very, very careful when stringing this bow up for the first time. It is the most likely of all the bows to come apart accidentally. Make sure to not exceed the safe length of draw of this bow, which is around half the length of the bow from nock to nock. For this bow, which is 56 inches nock to nock, 28 inches is the maximum draw. Wear protective gear when breaking this bow in. This bow is a challenge, but can be very rewarding. Enjoy your new bow!

Nomad - Finishing

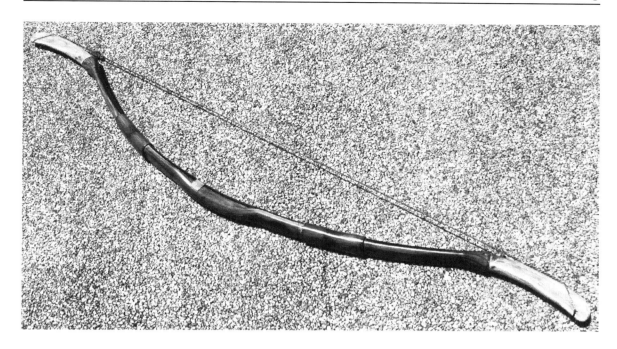

This bow was finished with a combination of liquid shoe polish and wood stain, all covered with a UV resistant clear coat spray. The back is brown shoe polish, the belly is a mix of mainly black with brown stripes.

The siyahs are finished with wood stain, applied in thin coats. By varying the direction of application a nice wood-like look can be achieved. Oil-based wood stain needs a couple days to fully dry before the clear coat can be applied.

Take-Down Archery

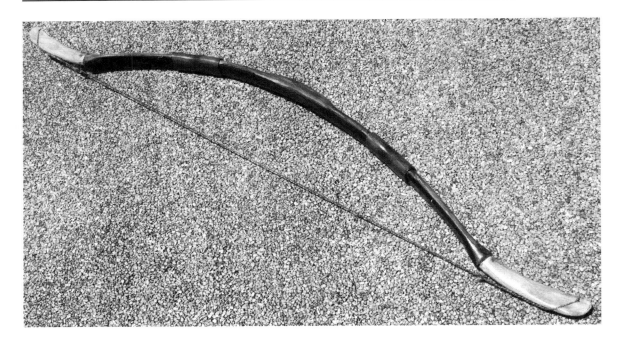

The belly of the bow is meant to mimic horn which is often used on the belly of Asiatic composite bows. The base is black shoes polish applied in layers until the shade is achieved, then blended with one coat of brown for depth followed by stripes of brown to give further depth.

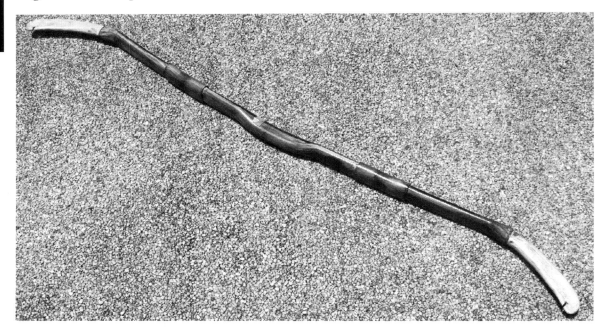

The back has a nice wood-like finish to it from the brown shoe polish. It is a very convincing finish from a distance. The connectors are dyed with brown shoe polish all around, darkened in the middle to mimic the look of bamboo with a node ground down.

Chapter Seven
Arrow Rest

An arrow rest is a platform that allows an arrow to sit in the same spot on the bow every time, which is important for consistent shooting. A rest or shelf also keeps the arrow in place while the bow is drawn and shot, protecting the bow hand and offering more stability. While not needed, a rest can help increase consistency and allows for good practice while also making a bow safer to use.

This rest is a simple version of what is known as a flip rest. It is made of thin plastic backed with foam mounting tape. This combination gives a very light rest that takes up little space and can fold completely flat to the bow if it needs to, while also dampening the sound of the arrow against the bow.

Using this rest allows you to use plastic vanes on your arrow, which have the added benefit of being water resistant. Used with almost any arrow, this rest will bring up your arrow speed versus shooting off the hand as well as help reduce the effects of arrow flex.

This one rest can be made for just about any traditional bow. It's a good idea to keep extras handy as they do not last forever.

Take-Down Archery

Start with a piece of thin plastic. PET (polyethylene) is a good plastic for this and can be found in plastic food containers, bottles, milk jugs and more. You want a plastic that is very thin and flexible.

Cut a rectangle of plastic, 3/4 inch wide and 1 and 1/2 inches long. Round the corners.

Chapter Seven - Arrow Rest

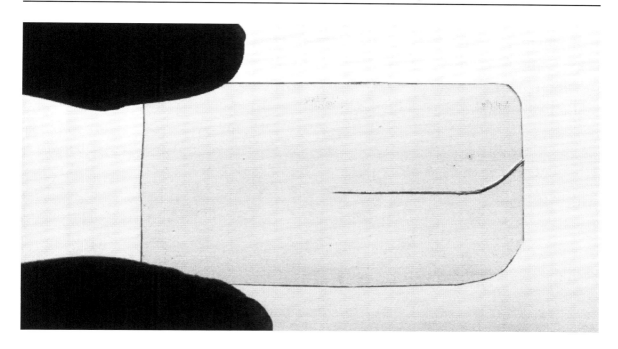

Make two cuts, following the picture above. The bottom cut will round off the bottom corner. The top cut should follow the bottom curve and then become a straight cut. Cut 3/4 inches into the rectangle.

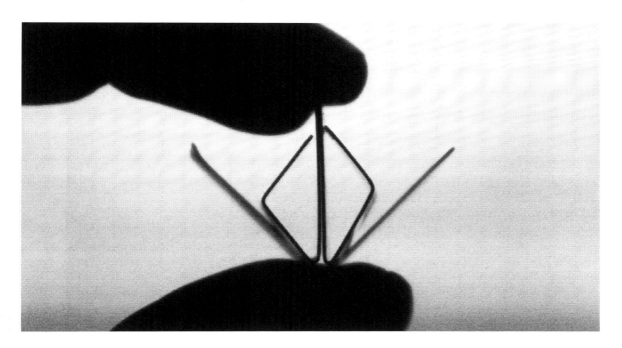

Now fold the rectangle in half. The direction you fold will depend on the handedness of your rest. The rest on the left is for a right handed bow and the right is for a left handed bow. Crease the top tab halfway so that it touches the main body of the plastic tab.

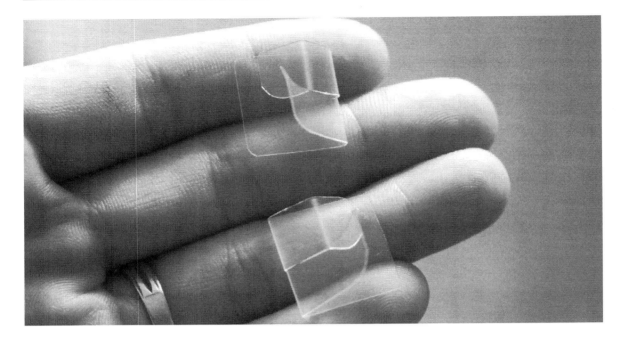

Here's another view of the shaped rests. The top is for a right handed bow, the bottom is for a left handed bow.

Cut a 3/4 inch square of double sided mounting tape. Keep the backing on the tape until you are ready to mount it to a bow. I like to keep a couple backups just in case the rest I'm using breaks or falls off the bow.

Chapter Seven - Arrow Rest

To mount it onto a bow, remove the backing and stick it on. The top, folded tab should sit where your arrows normally pass and the arrows will rest on the bottom curved tab.

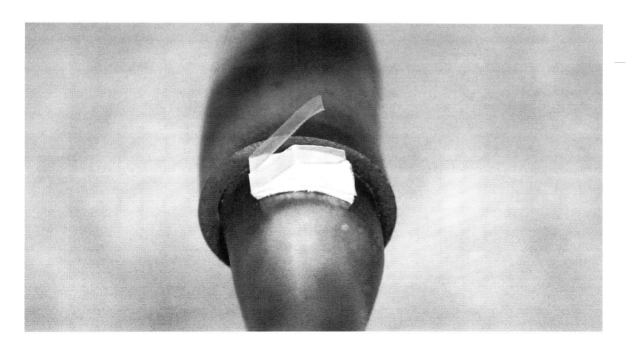

Make sure the rest is centered on the bow. The flexible plastic should conform to the handle of the bow. The flatter the handle, the better the rest will sit.

Take-Down Archery

To use the rest, place an arrow onto the lower curved tab. The little hook on the end is there to prevent the arrow falling from the rest.

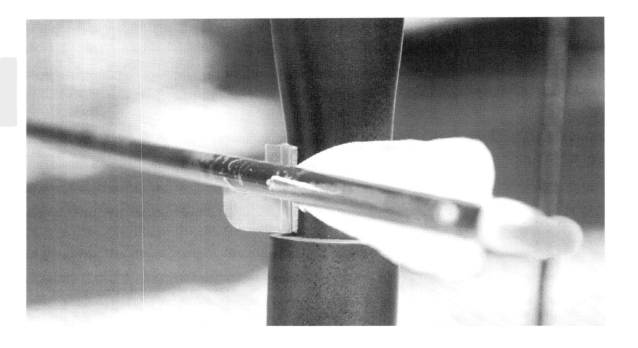

Adjust the top tab so that is pushes the arrow away from the bow just enough for the feathers or vanes to clear.

Chapter Seven - Arrow Rest

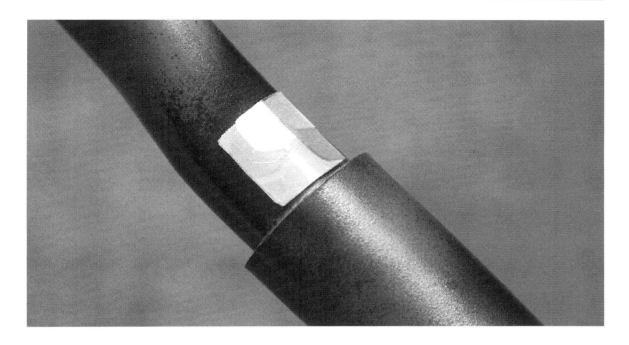

Here's the finished rest, installed and ready for use. While it will last a long time, it's always a good idea to have extras on hand in case it falls off or wears out.

Chapter Eight
Release Aid

Short bows like the ones in this book have a more acute string angle than longer bows. This means that when you are holding the bow at full draw with your fingers, your fingers are pinched in the angle the string makes. The shorter the bow, the more this can make shooting painful as well as a clean release of the string difficult.

The idea of using a release aid in the form of tabs, gloves and the like are very old. Even the use of solid rings of metal, ivory or stone as a means of augmenting the hand in drawing and releasing a bow are hundreds of years old. Today, mechanical releases are commonplace, especially for modern bows with very acute string angles.

The release aids in this chapter are simple, based on a design that originated back in the 1970's. They work as a hook, holding the string fixed until tension is taken off one side of the hook, resulting in a clean release. Because there is very little contact between string and release aid, string angle does not matter as much.

Another benefit of a release is avoiding the rub of the string over the fingertips and the amplified pressure of a thin string. Prolonged shooting can be painful especially without a glove or other covering over the fingers. The thick body of the release gives a good amount of cushion for the fingers and is less abrasive to the skin.

Release Aid - Design

There are three basic ways to build this style of release. The first, which is quite easy to shape and works very well, looks a little like the numbers 9 and 6. This style requires the use of only 2 fingers and works very well for lighter bows. The pictures on this page are actual size. The finger hole should be just a little larger than your middle finger.

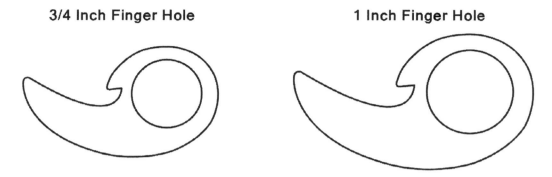

The next style allows a third finger to assist the other two in drawing the bow. The third finger not only increases your stability and ability to draw more weight, it also allows for better follow through and a more consistent release.

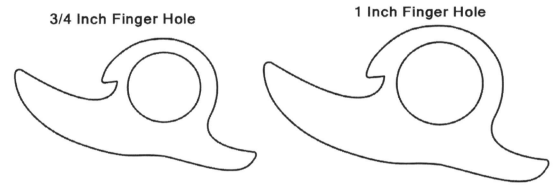

Finally this last style, which can be tricky to shape because of all the inside curves, is my personal favorite. It allows the use of three fingers while also giving a definite spot for the index finger to rest. This increases consistency between shots.

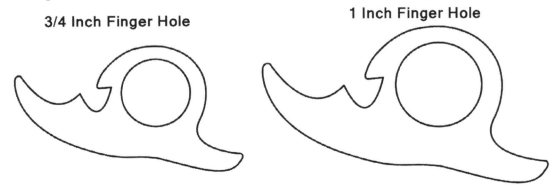

Take-Down Archery

Building

Making one of these releases is fairly straightforward. Now this does take some skill in carving, though PVC pipe is very easy to carve and can be worked with woodworking tools. For comfort, the release should be at least 1/4 of an inch thick.

In this section we'll go over how to prepare a piece of PVC pipe and turn it into a carveable slab. For a thicker slab, add another layer of PVC pipe. For extra decoration long the glue lines if using a clear glue, coat each side of the PVC pipe sheets with permanent marker prior to gluing. If using epoxy, commercial epoxy dyes can be used to stunning effect.

PVC works great for this as it is waterproof, easy to carve and holds up well, though other materials can be used. Dense woods like ebony, maple, hickory, osage and the like can be used alone or laminated for stunning effect. Bone, antler, horn, most synthetic composites and metal work as well.

Because the release is so light and small, it can be easily carried in a bag, pocket or any other container. It's also interesting-looking enough to be worn on the neck, just loop a length of cord or run a chain through the finger hole. I try to have a couple copies of the one I use most often with me, just in case.

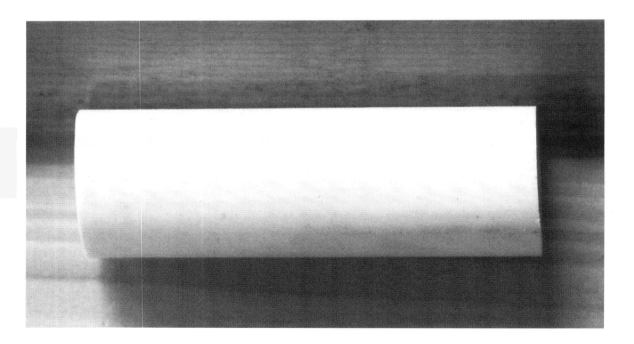

Cut a length of PVC pipe. If making 3/4 inch releases, use 1 inch pipe. Use 1 and 1/4 or larger pipe for 1 inch releases. Cut the pipe about an inch or two longer than the release you wish to make.

120

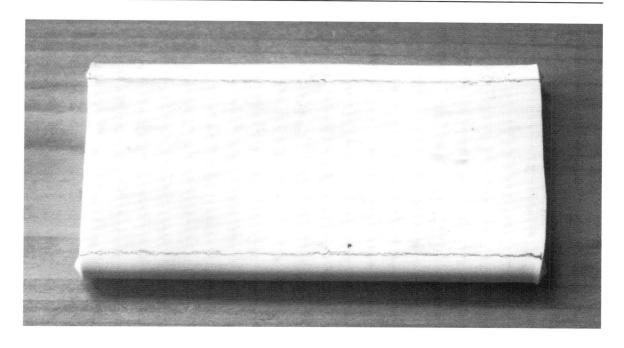

Flatten the pipe and then make a mark a little over 1/8 of an inch on the top and bottom edges of the pipe.

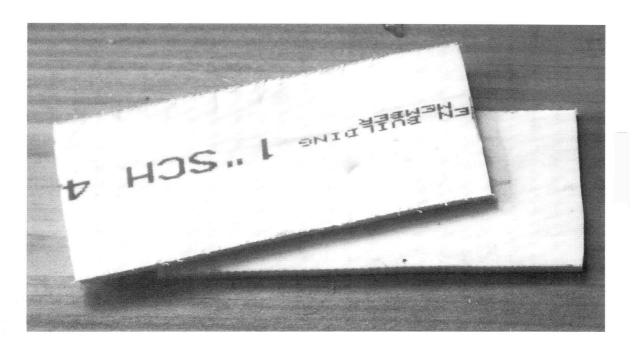

With a saw, cut the marked edges of the pipe. This will free the two sides of the pipe. With a sheet of sandpaper, knock off the rough edges and then roughen up the inside face of one sheet and the outside face of the other.

Take-Down Archery

Glue the two sanded edges together. A flexible glue like hot melt or any silicone based plastic cement work well. This gives you a nice 1/4 inch thick slab of PVC. Transfer the pattern of your choice on to the PVC slab.

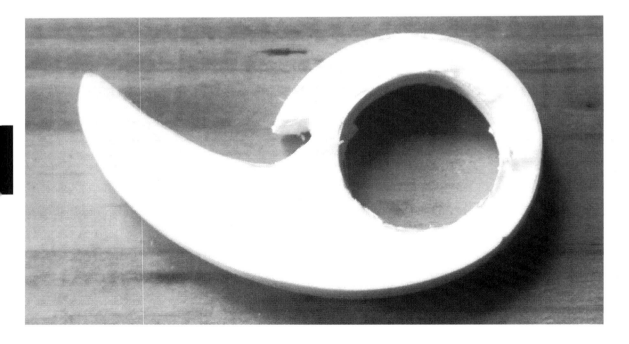

Drill the finger hole first with an appropriately sized spade bit. Make sure to be very careful and always clamp the workpiece to a stable surface before drilling. The rest of the shape can be freed with a coping saw or jeweler's saw.

Release Aid - Building

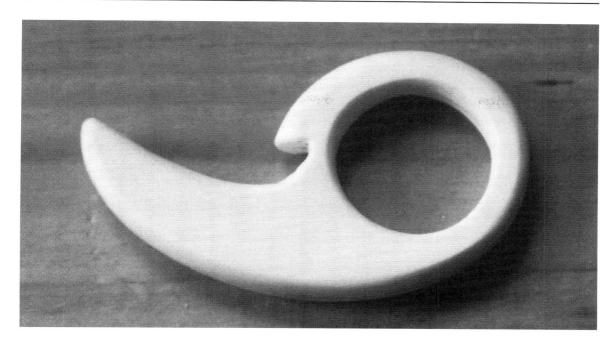

Using needle files and sandpaper, smooth the edges of the release. The inside of the ring can be smoothed with a dowel or smaller PVC pipe wrapped in sandpaper. With that finished, your release is ready for use. Make sure the little string hook is just slightly angled up to prevent string slips.

Shooting

Like anything else, shooting with a release takes practice. While the general motion and concept is similar to drawing a bow with fingers, it takes a little getting used to. I find that by locking the release behind the first joint of my fingers, I am able to consistently draw and hold a bow steady more so than with fingers alone.

One of the most important things to remember is to keep the index finger firmly locked during the whole draw. If your index finger slips at all, the string could easily pop out of the hook while you are in the middle of the draw. Because it is such a sudden release, your hand could whip backward into your face. The arrow may also go where you don't want it to.

In this section we'll go over how to use the release and then finish up with a few parts of a shot progression. If using a three-finger release aid, it can also be used with the ring finger over the main tab. In this way the index finger pulls the small tab like a trigger to fire the bow. It's a little trickier and prone to slipping so that method is not pictured here.

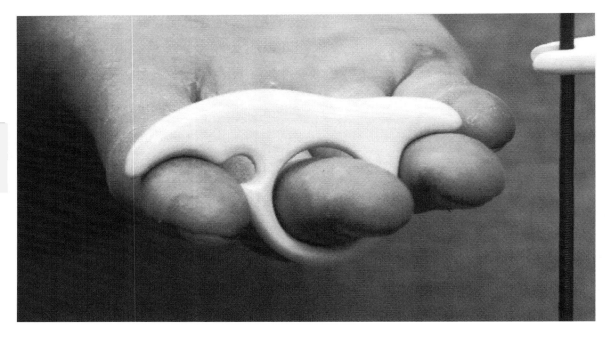

With your shooting hand palm up, place the release on your middle finger with the main body of the ring facing upwards. The larger side with the string hook should rest on your index finger. If your release has a secondary lever on it, that rests on your ring finger.

Release Aid - Shooting

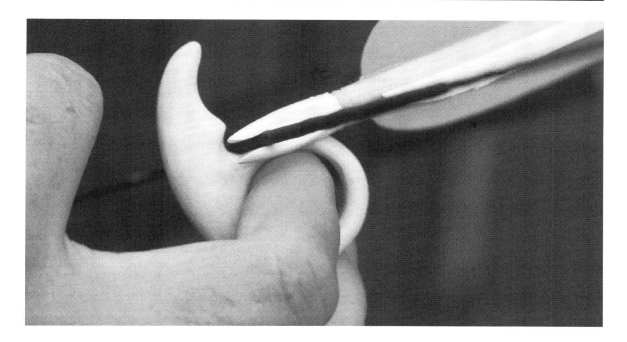

Hold the release with the first knuckle of your fingers. To use it, slide the release onto the bowstring just below the arrow. The hook will grip on to the string.

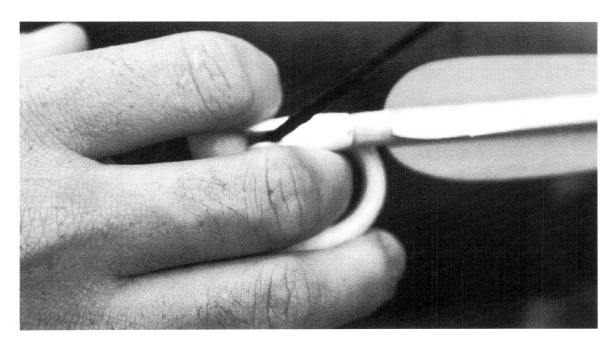

Place your index finger on the release and hold the release with the index finger pulled more than the other two. This will keep the string in the release. Do not let the index finger creep forward when drawing or the string may slip and you may not only accidentally fire the bow but may hit yourself in the face.

Take-Down Archery

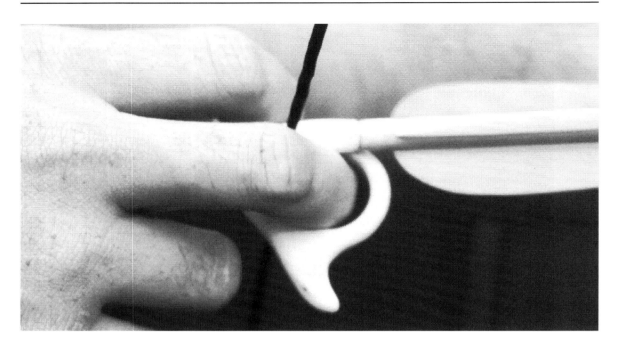

If your release does not have a second lever, simply use the index and middle fingers to draw the string.

To release or fire the bow, simply point your index finger as if pointing to your target. The release will rotate around the middle finger and the string will be released. In the next 3 pictures, I'll show you a shot progression.

Release Aid - Shooting

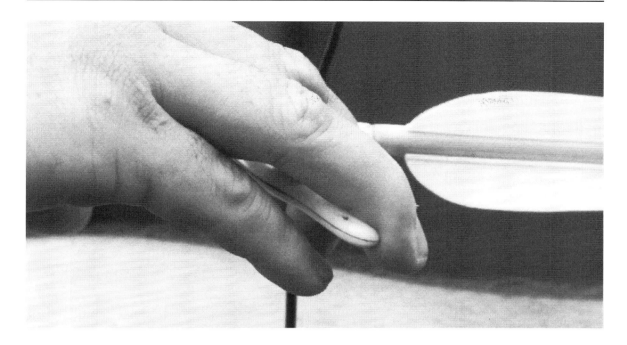

I start with the string in the hook. My index finger is pulled back, ensuring the string does not slip off the release.

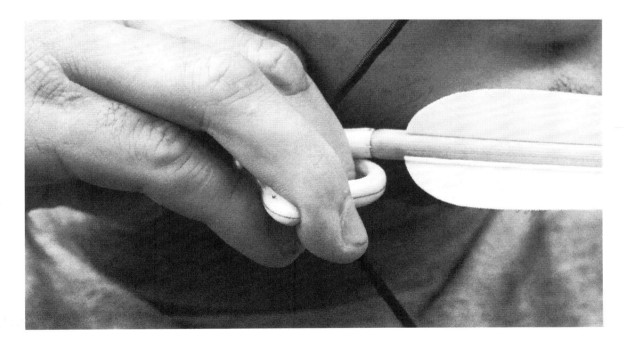

I draw back to my anchor point. You should draw to the same anchor point you use with fingers. Once at full draw, keep the index finger drawn back and don't let your hand creep forward.

Take-Down Archery

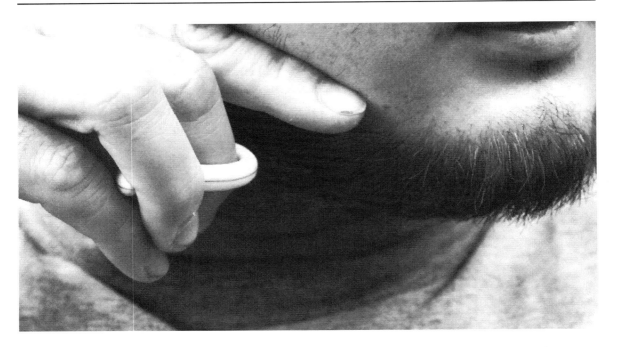

I lift my index finger and point. The arrow and string whip forward and the release rotates. Notice how my hand is pulled back slightly. It is a good idea to follow through with the release to keep from dropping your hand forward and slowing down the arrow.

Chapter Nine
Take Down Arrows

Arrows are one of the three parts of a bow setup. While the best bows can make use of any arrow, the best arrows make a poor bow shoot well. It is the arrow that ultimately determines how effective your setup is. A well-matched arrow can increase the speed and power of a bow as well as ensure greater accuracy and dependability.

No matter how small your bow breaks down, your pack or setup is limited by the length of your arrows. While solid, one-piece arrows are usually much safer to use, they can be cumbersome to pack especially if your bow breaks down into two or more pieces. Though there are many methods to take down arrows, this chapter goes over two simple and strong methods that can be easily and safely done by most.

The most important thing in building take-down arrows is to start with a dependable and sturdy arrow that works for your bow. It is important to shoot the arrow, just as you would shoot a bow before breaking it down. Get to know how it flies and if it works well with your bow.

While these arrows are dependable and strong if made correctly, they need to be checked after every shot. An arrow travels very fast and very close to your hand. Take down arrows work best with an arrow rest.

Carbon and Aluminum

The standard for arrows today are carbon with aluminum considered the old standby. When it comes to PVC bows, both have their advantages and disadvantages. Both are similar in that they use standardized point inserts which makes them versatile. They are also stable when it comes to moisture and water, which may be a deciding factor if your pack is near water or in a humid environment.

Carbon, which has become the mainstay of modern archery, has its merits. It's very tough, light and does not take a bend. One of its best qualities is the ability to stabilize quickly and resist vibration. This makes carbon very accurate, all other things equal. On the downside, carbon arrows are sometimes too light and don't make the most of a PVC bow's power. They can also shatter and splinter when they do break. One way to increase weight and resist breakage is to glue on a piece of slightly larger aluminum arrow shaft over the point, much like in the bonus track.

Aluminum on the other hand is usually a little heavier but tends to be whippy if the spine or stiffness is not matched to the bow properly. They tend to bend if they hit something hard rather than break and usually snap cleanly when they do break. The added weight of aluminum arrows make them better suited for PVC bows.

When making take downs, aluminum and carbon work best in 3 pieces. The arrow is just as tough as a solid arrow because the area of most stress has no joint.

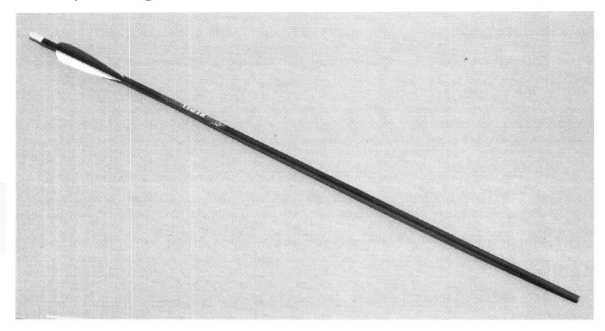

Start with your carbon or aluminum shaft. Mark the places you will cut the shaft. 3 pieces is what I usually do as the center of the arrow is under the most stress. Mark either halfway for 2 pieces or thirds for 3 pieces.

Take Down Arrows - Carbon and Aluminum

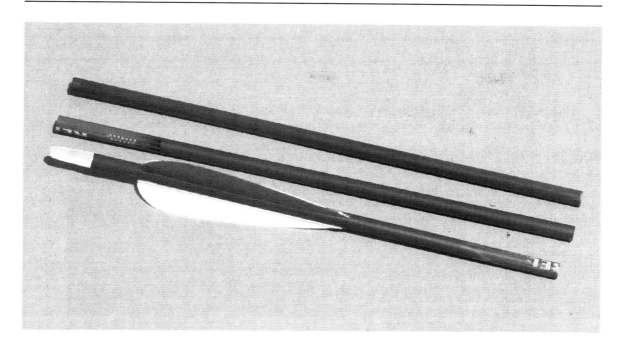

Cut along your marks. If you are close to an archery shop, most will cut the shafts for you. If cutting them yourself, either use a powered cut-off disk or a hacksaw. Be careful with the dust from cutting and wear the appropriate protection.

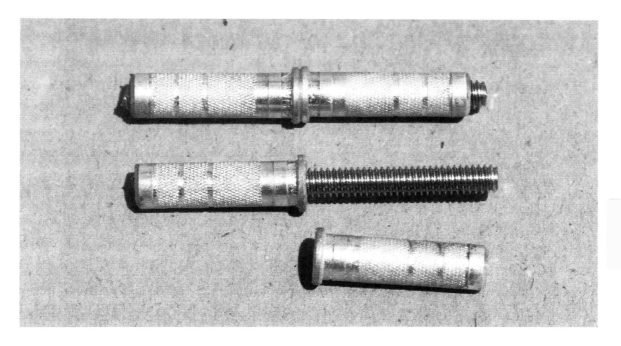

You will use 2 pairs of connectors for a 3 piece arrow and 1 pair for a 2 piece. The connector assembly consists of two point inserts and a 8-32 threaded rod cut just a hair longer than the two connectors. Glue the threads with a bit of hot melt or thread locker on the left side so that the other side can come off easily.

Take-Down Archery

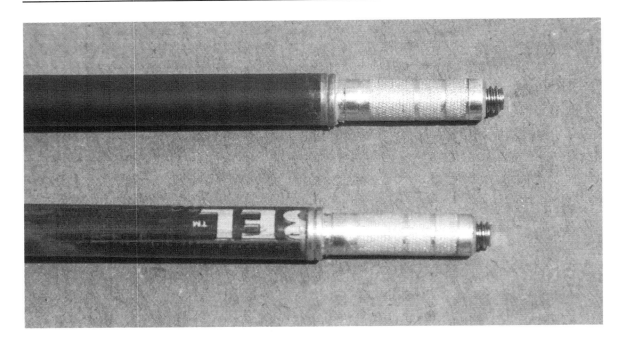

Glue connector into the front ends of the tubes, the sides that are closest to the arrow point. Make sure the connector your glue in first has the threading that is not locked. Tighten the other connector.

Glue the second connector into its corresponding section of arrow, essentially putting the arrow back together. The connector should be tight beforehand sot hat the arrow comes back together the way it was cut.

Take Down Arrows - Carbon and Aluminum

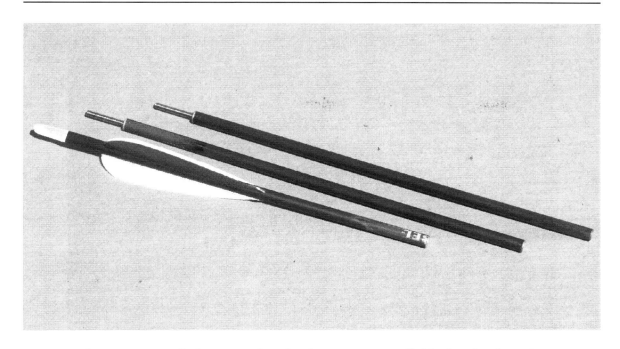

When unscrewed, the arrow breaks down very small. Notice the threads are sticking out of the rear or each section. This allows an arrow to be lengthened by screwing an extra piece into the point section of an arrow. It's a good way to make an expedient arrow for fishing.

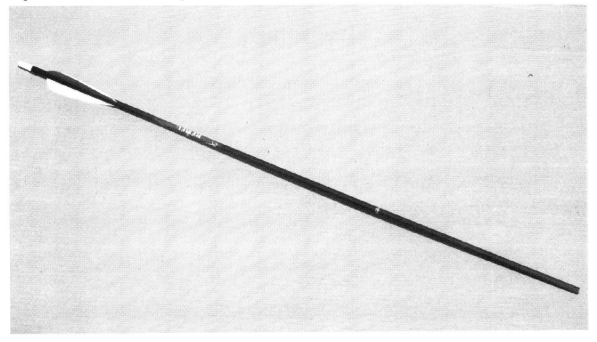

Here's the assembled arrow. It's a good idea to number the pieces so that this arrow's pieces won't get mixed up with another arrow if they are all kept in the same container.

Wood

Wood has been an arrow material for quite some time. While not as tough or durable as carbon and aluminum and definitely not as resistant to long exposure to moisture, wood is still a viable option. Wood arrows are typically heavier than other arrow types and do a good job at helping PVC bows perform more efficiently.

On the flip side, they are prone to warping and changing in size with temperature and humidity even with a good finish. This can cause problems with the take down sleeves. Wood arrows, being natural products, tend to vary quite a bit in weight from arrow to arrow and need more careful adjustment. They can also loose their straightness and require straightening from time to time.

Despite these downfalls, I personally prefer wood arrows. When buying wood arrows, make sure they are spined to your bow's weight and buy from a reputable seller. Good quality wood arrows can be very consistent, accurate, tough, straight and incredibly forgiving. Poor arrows can be inconsistent, soft or brittle, warped and may even break and cause injury. Good wood species are Port Orford Cedar, Sitka Spruce, Lodgepole Pine, Yellow Poplar and Ash. Especially when making take down arrows, get the best quality you can.

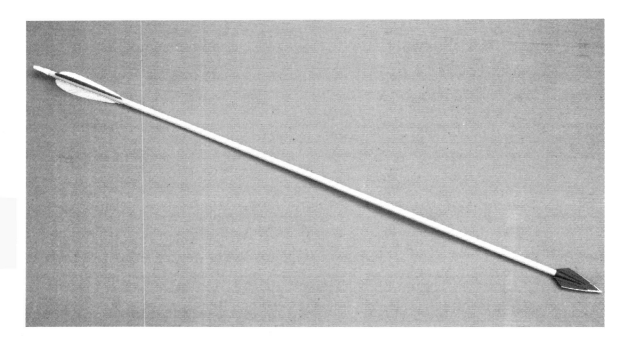

Start with your wooden arrow. This method usually only works with a shaft that is uniform along its length and may not work on tapered or barreled shafts.

Take Down Arrows - Wood

Cut the shaft in half with a 45 degree cut. This will ensure that both sides of the cut can seat together. It forms a sort of self-aligning joint.

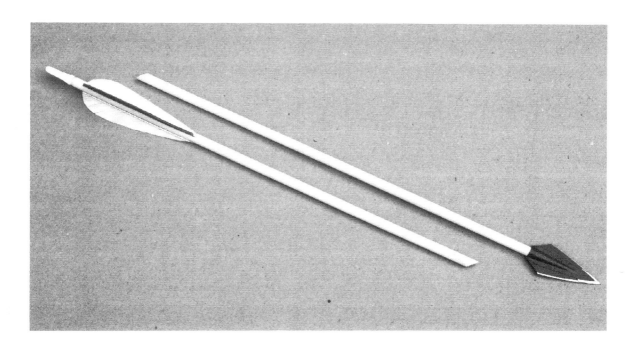

Here are the 2 parts. If you want a 3 piece arrow, then measure the arrow into thirds and cut the arrow accordingly.

Take-Down Archery

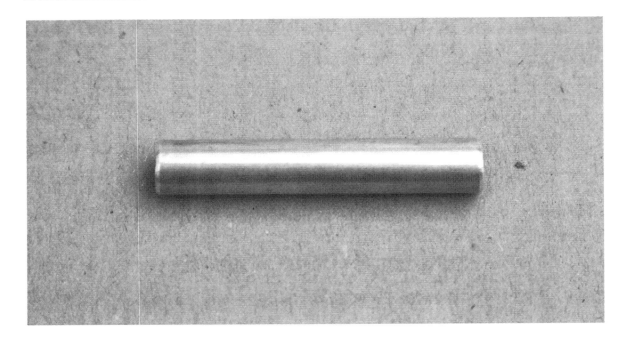

Cut a brass tube that is one size above your arrow's diameter. For 5/16 arrows, use an 11/32 tube and for 11/32 arrow use a 3/8 tube. Sand the edges to make them smooth so they will transition smoothly from arrow to connector.

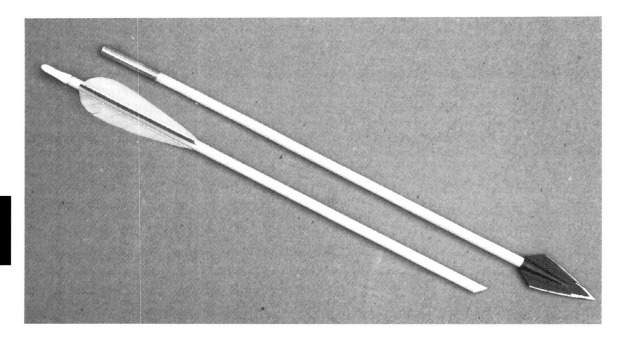

Glue the connector onto the rear of the front section of arrow. This should be very snug but not tight that the shaft is damaged. Leave half of the connector empty so that the back half of the arrow has a good amount of contact with the connector.

Take Down Arrows - Wood

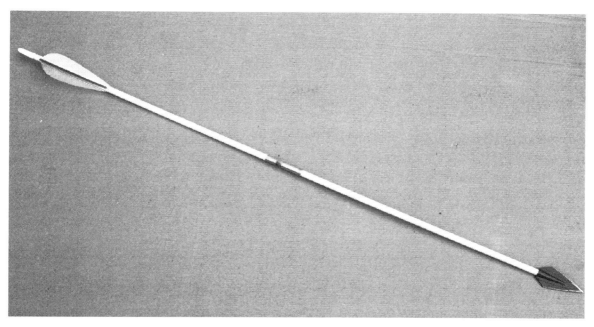

    Rub a little beeswax onto the rear end of the arrow and slide it into the connector. The wax will help prevent the rear getting stuck while also helping keep the pieces together. The arrow can now be used as normal. Just keep in mind that the arrow needs to be gripped from the front half when extracting from a target or the arrow will come apart.

Take-Down Archery

Fletching Jig

A fletching jig is an important tool to accurately and consistently place feathers or vanes on an arrow. Depending on your personal preference, you may want to shoot feathers as opposed to plastic vanes or vice versa. A fletching jig will allow you to put new feathers or vanes on an arrow, or let you fletch your own arrows.

This jig is fairly simple and allows for a good amount of adjustment to fletch an arrow in 2, 3, 4, 6, 8 and 12 vane configurations. While this type of jig is mainly for straight-fletching, a little bit of offset can be achieved by positioning the leading edge of the clamp to the left or right.

This jig can be modified in a number of ways. By gluing the clothespins on to a thin board or rigid sheet (like flattened PVC pipe), the jig can be made very compact and is perfect for fletching in the field. The feather clamp shown is also great for holding feathers if you are stripping and grinding raw feathers yourself.

If you cannot find thin-walled pipe for the feather clamp, schedule 40 will work. You will just need to adjust the clothespin jaws to fit the thicker feather clamp. A simple way to do this is to wrap a dowel in sandpaper and sand the inside of the jaws of each clothespin. Keep sanding until the feather clamp fits snugly into the top of the jaw.

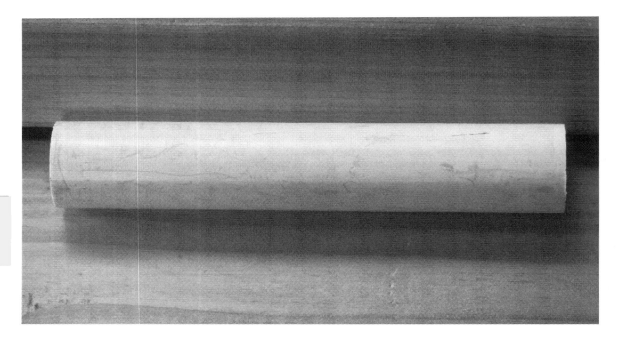

To build a feather clamp, start with a 6 inch length of 3/4 inch, SDR-21 pipe. This is thin-wall pipe, commonly used for irrigation. If you plan on using feathers longer than 5 and 1/4 inches long, start with a longer pipe, leaving an extra 3/4 inch over your feather length. For example, for 6 inch feathers use a 6 and 3/4 inch pipe.

Take Down Arrows - Fletching Jig

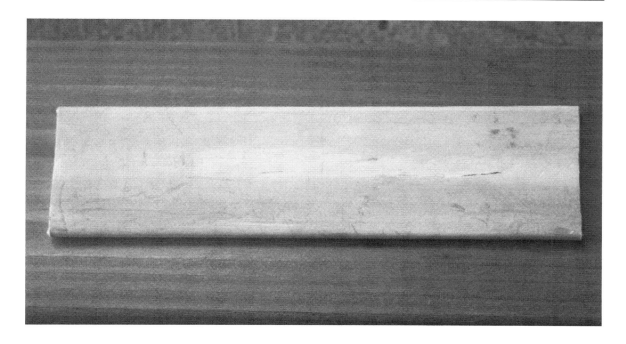

Heat the pipe and completely flatten it. Make sure the boards you use to flatten are true or the flattened pipe may end up with some flex.

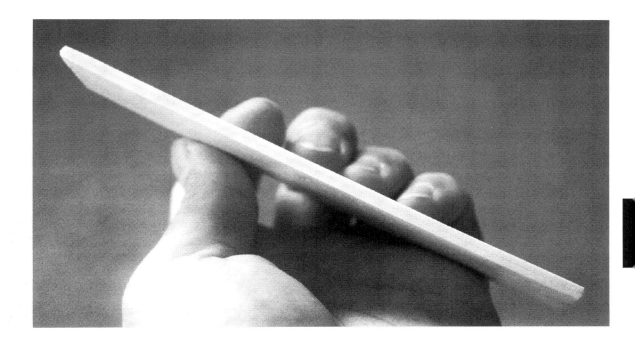

Grind down one edge until a very fine line appears and the side wall has been completely cut through.

Take-Down Archery

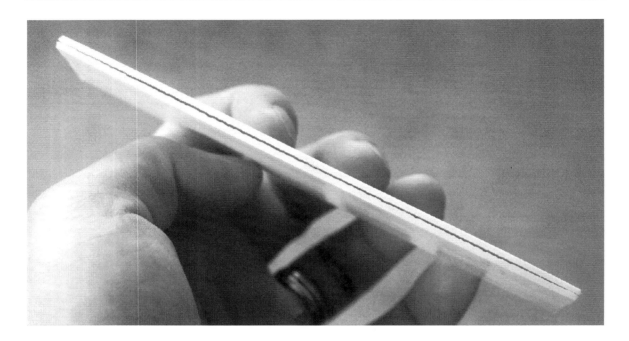

Gently heat the pipe until there is a slight separation between the two sides. This should be no wider than a sheet of paper is thick.

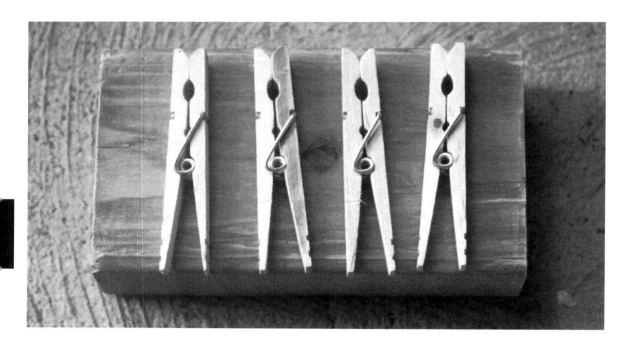

For the main body of the clamp, start with a 2x4 the same length as your feather clamp, or 6 inches if you are following this build. You will need 4 wooden clothespins as well. If building a single clamp, you only need 2 clothespins.

Take Down Arrows - Fletching Jig

Glue the clothespins to the 2x4, placing one on each corner, lined up to the bottom and outside edge of the block. This is the main body of the fletching jig.

To establish the proper angles for 2, 3 and 4 fletched arrows, we'll be using a hex nut. Find a bolt that will go over the end of the arrows you will be fletching. You can either place it on an arrow or a length of the same diameter dowel.

Take-Down Archery

Open two of the clothespins on one side of the clamp and place the dowel into the jaws. The clothespins will hold the dowel in place.

Using the hex nut as a guide, draw a line from the center of the dowel out to each point of the hex nut. These lines will serve as a way to measure the angles of fletch.

Take Down Arrows - Fletching Jig

Your fletching jig is now ready to use. As is, this jig can do two arrow at one time. If using glue, it's a good idea to make two feather clamps so both can be drying at the same time.

Fletching An Arrow

It's a good idea to know how to fletch an arrow. Whether you're fixing up existing fletching, switching fletching type or fletching your own arrows to save that cost, knowing how to fletch an arrow can be useful. The fletching jig in the last section can be used for both feather and vanes.

Plastic vanes are great if you arrows will be near water as they are weatherproof. While they are not as forgiving as feathers, they will work fairly well as long as an arrow rest is used. Vanes work best in a normal 3-fletch configuration.

Feathers, while they can be susceptible to moisture, are much more forgiving to shoot. They fold down rather than kick off things, which can reduce deflection of arrows both on the bow and during flight. Feathers also have a natural curve that can be worked with to impart spin on an arrow, allowing it to stabilize faster.

We'll be fletching with 3 feathers using the fletching jig we made. Plastic vanes will work in this way as well. If you want to try different arrangements for feathers, you can use 2 to as many as 12 feathers. The more feather the more drag. This can be a benefit if you are shooting in limited space and you don't want your arrows to go very far.

Let's get started.

We'll be fletching two arrows, so place an arrow into each of the pairs of clothespins. They should set into the middle of the jaw's groove, don't try to push them lower or higher. This will keep them more consistent.

Take Down Arrows - Fletching an Arrow

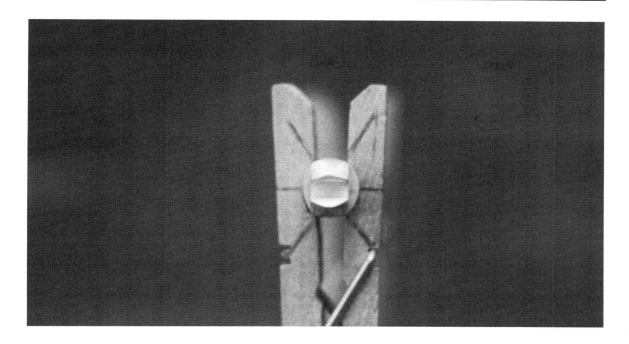

Looking from the end, we'll position the arrow based on the nock. Line the nock up to the horizontal line, like in the picture.

This is how the feather clamp should sit on top of the arrow. Without a feather or vane in the clamp, it should be slightly loose between the top of the clothespin jaws. Mark the back end of the clamp where it touches the clothespin and then wherever you want your feather to start.

Take-Down Archery

Place a feather or vane into the feather clamp. The pipe should hold the feather in place without any need for outside clamping force. For feathers, slide the clamp over the feather from the front until the rear of the feather lines up with the index mark we made. Place a thin line of glue on the base of feather or vane. Household cement or superglue both work.

Press the clamp down onto the arrow. Make sure the feather is lined up before setting it in place. Follow your glue of choice for drying time before moving on.

Take Down Arrows - Fletching an Arrow

Once the glue has dried, remove the feather clamp. Here's the first feather in place.

Rotate the arrow until the nock is aligned with the one of the diagonal sets of lines. This will set the arrow up for the second feather, 120 degrees away from the first. The attached feather should rest between lines like in the picture.

Take-Down Archery

Here's the second feather applied.

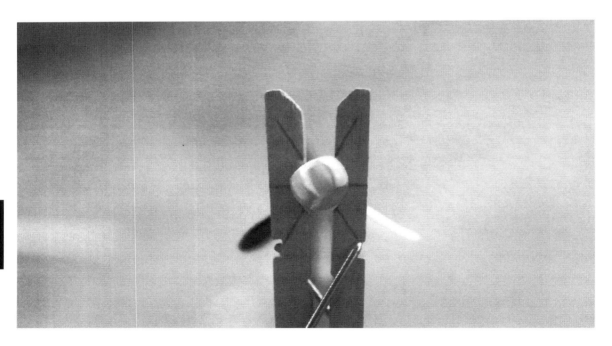

Rotate the arrow again. This time, the nock should line up with the other diagonal line. The other two feathers should rest as close as possible to the center between lines. Because of the curve feather have to them, rely more on the position of the nock than the feathers. Vanes will be more precise.

Take Down Arrows - Fletching an Arrow

Here's the final feather applied.

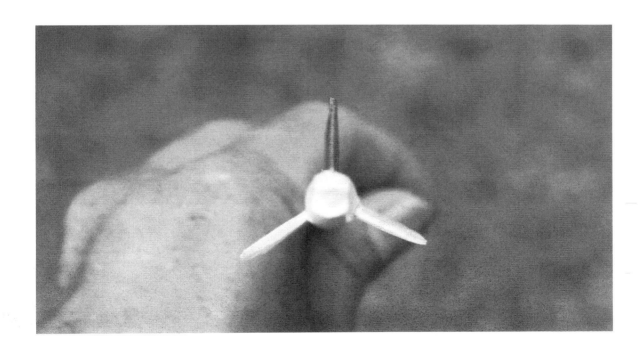

From the end, here is the finished fletching. The feathers should be 120 degrees apart from each other.

Take-Down Archery

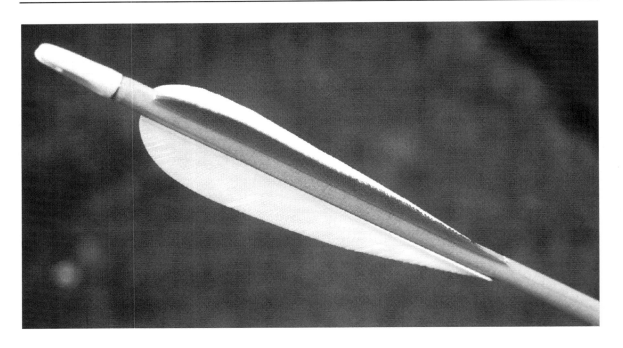

Here is another view of the finished fletching. By using a combination of nock alignments, the jig can be used for 2, 3, 4, 6, 8 and 12 fletch configurations.

Chapter Ten
String Building

    The bow string is one of the three essential parts of a bow setup. Without the string, a bow is lifeless. It is the string that transfer's a bow's energy to the arrow. While most any strong cord will serve as a string, using a string that eats up energy will bring down your entire setup. On the flip side, a cord too weak could cause injury if it breaks while the bow is at full draw.
    A string that is well-made, strong and low-stretch will bring out the best of your bow in terms of speed and efficiency. If you do choose to stretchier materials, keep in mind that they will work, but can cut a lot of speed from your bow. Another side effect of having a stretchy string is extra arm slap from the string stretching and striking your hand after each shot.
    In this chapter we'll be building an endless loop string as well as some tools to make building strings easier and more consistent. An endless loop string can be made with many types of low-stretch materials including Dacron and Fast Flight bow string material and non-archery specific materials like Dacron fishing line, Dyneema dental floss and others.

Serving Jig

Building an endless loop string requires the individual strands of string be lashed or served together. While this can be done by hand, it helps to have a tool that feeds string and keeps up a high amount of tension. This will result in cleaner, tighter servings that are not likely to pull out with normal use.

This is a very simple serving jig that using tension from a nut and bolt to feed serving thread quickly and evenly onto a bow string. The dimensions here will work for most standard spools of bow string serving thread that are 2 inches long, 1 and 3/8 inches in diameter with a 5/16 inch hole. You can wrap thread around a 2 inch long tube or simply change the dimensions of the serving jig to fit an different spool.

The thread should be very heavy, around 0.02 inches or more. This type of thread is used a lot for sewing awnings, outdoor upholstery, saddles and shoes leather. A good place to find this size of thread is from leather or upholstery shops. If you are using more modern string materials like Dyneema, spectra or fast flight, you will want to serve you string with the same as these materials may wear or slice through the softer nylon.

Cut a length of 3/4 inch, schedule 40 PVC pipe 5 and 1/4 inches long. Make a mark 1 and 1/2 inches in from both ends. This will result in a 2 and 1/4 inner section like the picture above.

String Building - Serving Jig

Flatten the pipe and mark a 1/4 inch on both edges. The pipe needs to be completely flattened.

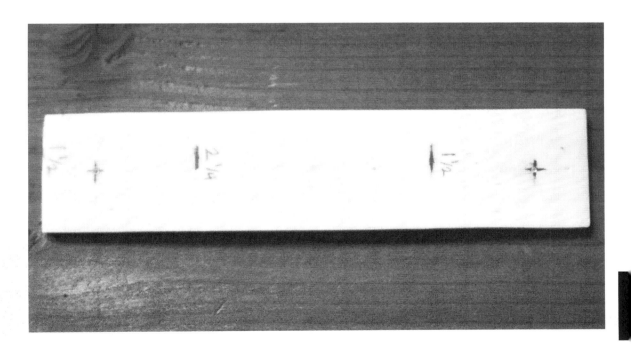

Cut the top and bottom edges from the pipe and put one slab of PVC aside. This can make a second serving jig. Measure 1/2 an inch in from both ends, centered along the sheet of PVC. Also mark the very center of the sheet.

Take-Down Archery

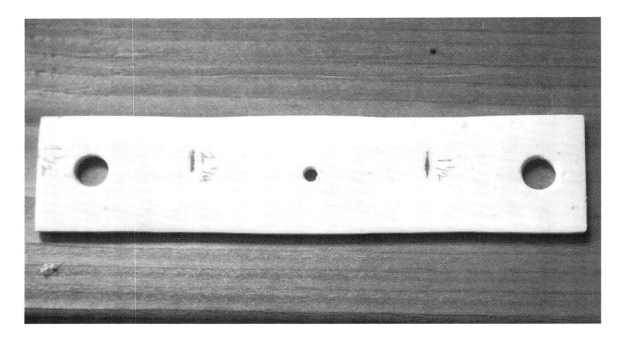

Drill a 5/16 inch hole on each end on the marks. Drill a 1/8 inch hole in the very center of the PVC sheet. With a sharp knife or sandpaper, break the inside edges of the drilled holes to remove any sharp edges.

Heat the PVC and bend it at a 90 degree angle on the inside of each 1 and 1/2 inch mark. The end of a 2x4 works very well for this.

String Building - Serving Jig

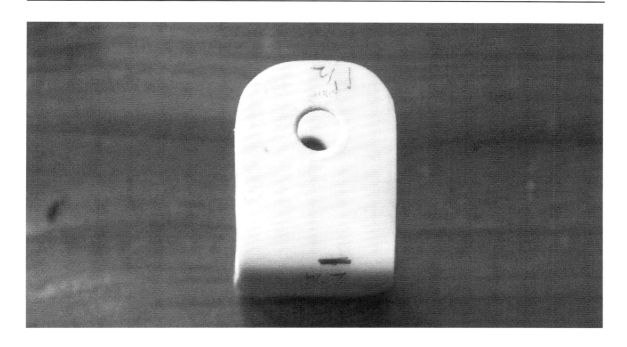

Round off the edges of the serving jig. They don't need to be so deeply curved, the square edges just need to blunted.

With a tile saw or nock file, cut two grooves across the serving jig. The lines should intersect at the 1/8 inch hole in the middle of the server. These will allow the server to hug the string while the server is used. One direction allows for more speed while serving open string and the other allows for serving in tight spots.

Take-Down Archery

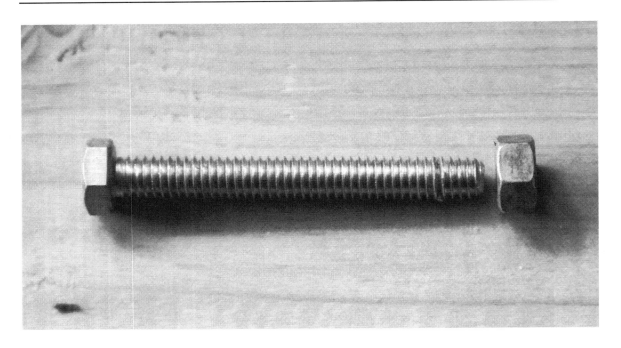

A 2 and 1/2 inch long, 5/16 inch hex bolt and hex nut will be used to complete the serving jig and hold the serving spool in place. Instead of a hex nut, a wing nut could also be used. This would make quick adjustment quicker and easier.

Here's the finished and assembled serving jig. Place the serving spool between the two arms of the server and pass the bolt through. Then tighten the nut until everything is tight. Thread the loose end of serving string through the center hole and your serving jig is ready to go.

String Jig

In order to build an endless loop string, you will need some sort of jig to support the strands as the string is served or wrapped together. A jig will keep up good tension and allow work to be done on different parts of the string without changing its length or balance.

This jig is very simple, but with a little practice can be used to build top-quality strings very quickly. The body of the jig can be built on any board or strong support like a wall or edge of a door, etc. The length of your board is determined by the string you want to build. Your board should be at least as long as the longest string you want to build.

To keep things from getting too confusing, your string length will be around 3-4 inches shorter than your bow's length. And this is the bow's length from nock to nock, not tip to tip. So when building a string for say, a 48 inch pipe that became a 46 inch nock to nock bow, take away 3 inches. This string will be 43 inches long, but once it's on the bow, will be around 42 and 1/2 inches.

In order to keep from getting confused, it's a good idea to mark both string and bow length on your jig.

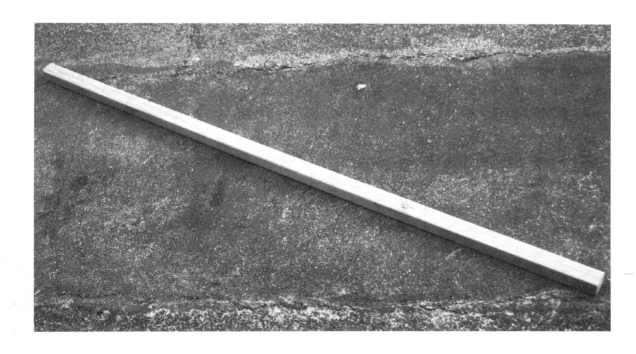

Start with a 2x2 or 2x4, 3 inches longer than your longest string will be. The longest string for the jig in the picture is 57 inches, so the board is 60 inches long.

Take-Down Archery

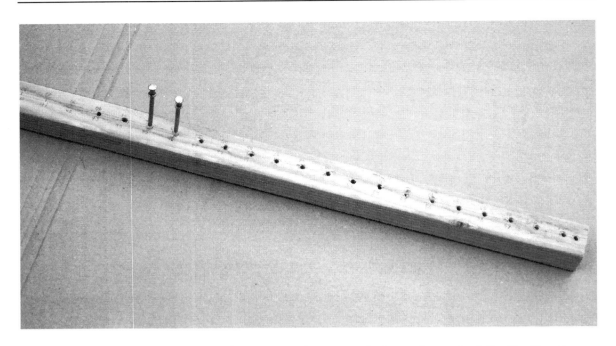

Measure your string marks starting from 1 inch from the end of the jig. Starting 5 inches below the shortest string you will build, place a mark every inch. Starting from the shortest string length you will build, drill 3/16 inch holes, 1 inch deep and at each inch line.

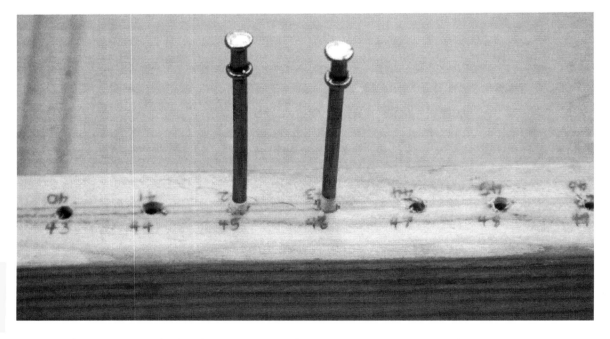

Place two 3 inch duplex nails an inch apart. These are what the string material will wrap around. You can see there are two different sets of numbers. The set on the bottom is the bow length and will be 3 inches larger than the actual measurement. The top set is the actual measurement of the strings.

String Building - String Jig

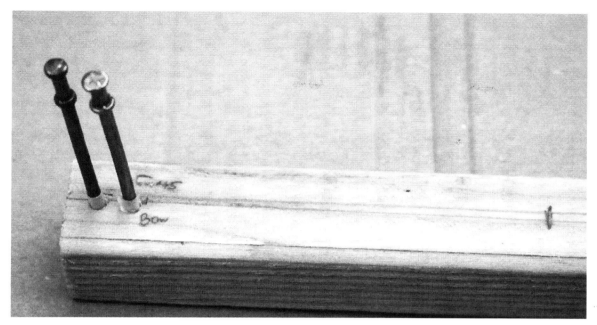

Drill two holes at the beginning of the jig, one 1/2 an inch from the end and one 1 inch away. Mark the board 5 inches from the 1 inch hole from the end. That mark allows you to match up loop servings. I have marked my jig string on the top so I know those measurements are for string length and bow on the bottom to make a string for a particular bow.

Endless Loop

The endless loop or continuous loop string is a fairly simple and very durable style of bowstring. It's relatively quick to build, is simple to keep consistent and is very efficient. While the jig (which is already quite simplified) makes building strings of a certain length simple, with practice these strings can be built with as little as a couple nails in a log.

When it comes to an endless string, the individual strands need to be small enough to fit at least 10 strands to one 1/8 inch thick bow string. This can be achieved with purpose-made archery string material like Dacron and Fast Flight. Other alternatives like Dacron, polyester and spectra fishing lines, commercial thickness Dacron stitching thread, dental floss as well as others can also be used.

Keep in mind that the combined breaking strength of all the strands need to be about 4 to 5 times the weight of your bow at full draw. It's also a good idea to stay away from using nylon and any thread that is too thin. If it takes over 20 strands to make a full-sized bowstring, the thread may be too small.

The first time may be difficult, but once you get the hang of it, it takes little time to make many bowstrings. It's a good idea to always carry a spare string or two to fit the bow you're using.

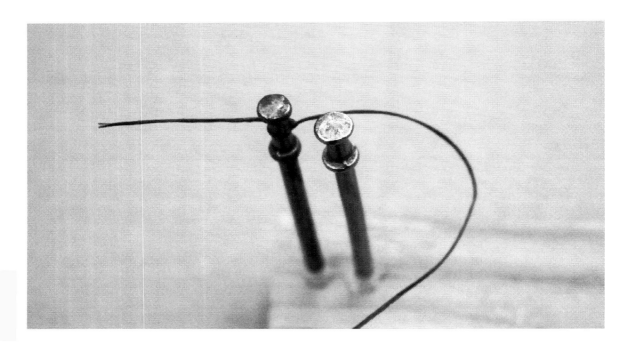

Start by tying the end of your string material to the back nail on the starting end of the string jig. Make sure this knot is secure as the cord will be under pressure.

String Building - Endless Loop

Run the cord from the first nail to the third. Place this nail where you want the length of your string to be from the end of one loop to the other. Place the fourth nail an inch away.

Keep wrapping around the second and third nail until you have as many strands as you need. If using Dacron or Fast Flight, 14-16 strands are usually enough for most bows. As a rule of thumb, I make my strings to be around 1/8 of an inch in diameter when all strands are held together. Always end on the fourth nail, making an even number of strands.

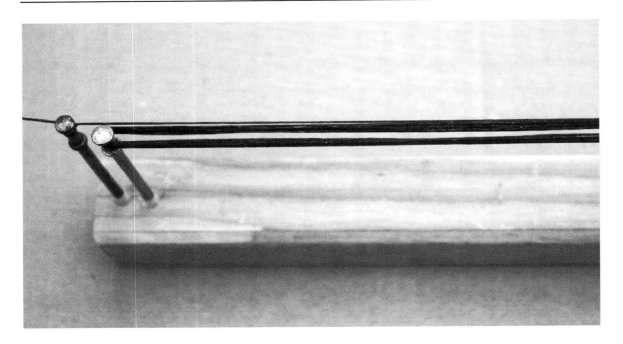

Make sure both ends and all the wrapped strands are tight. Go back and ensure both of the tied ends are secure before continuing.

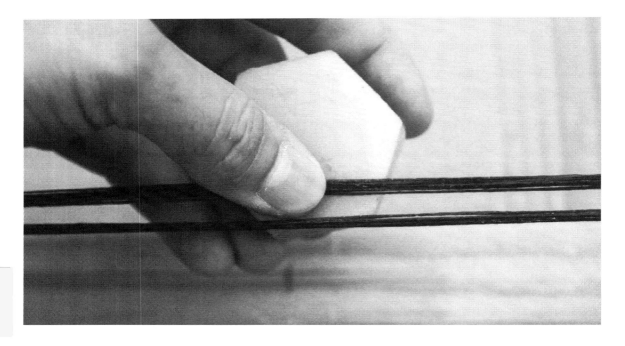

Starting at the 5 inch line on the jig, wax the first bundle, the one with the two loose ends. You should make sure that wax covers ever strand for about 4 inches, or the length of your string loop plus an inch.

String Building - Endless Loop

To start serving the string, pull some thread out of the serving jig. Take the loose end and pass it through the middle of the bundle of strands. Make sure the end is lined up with the 5 inch mark on the board and begin wrapping around the string from that point.

After a few wraps, the thread should be secure. Twist the spool until the serving jig butts up against the string. Twist in the direction of your wrapping and the server will lay down the thread tightly. Start with the server like in the picture to clear the other string bundle and wrap until you cover about 1/2 an inch of string.

Take-Down Archery

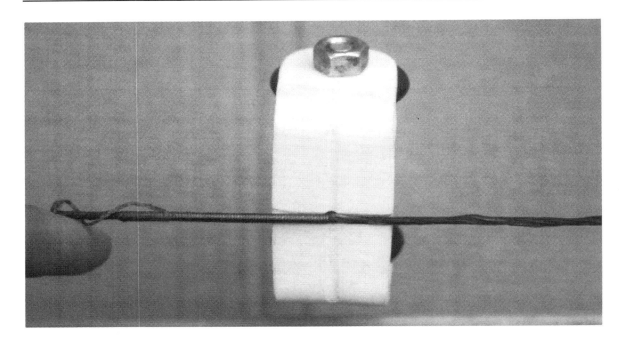

Pull the loose thread back and keep spinning the server. To get through this stretch quickly, turn the server like the picture above. This will give you a little more speed.

Keep serving until you reach 3 and 1/2 inches. This is where we'll finish the serving with a simple reverse-serve.

String Building - Endless Loop

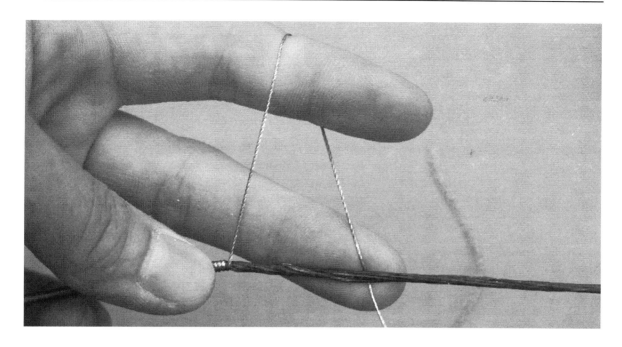

Cut about 10 inches of thread from the spool. In the same direction as the wrap, loop the end of the thread over an outstretched finger and over the other side like the picture.

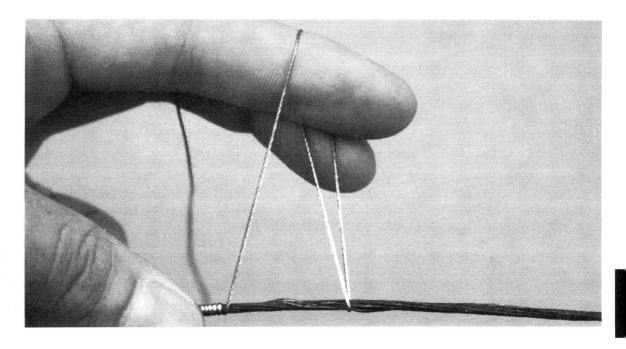

Bring the loose end up and into the loop. Move in the same clockwise or counterclockwise direction as you were before around the string, except go back toward the beginning of the wrap.

Take-Down Archery

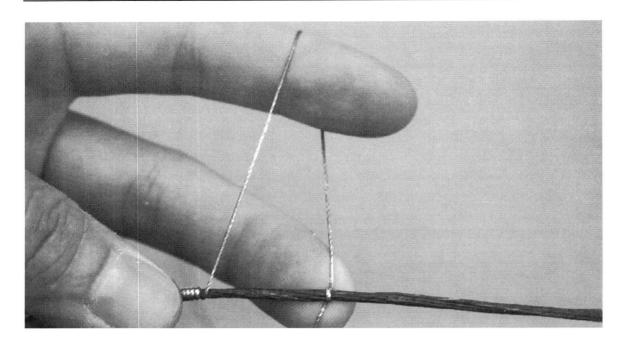

Complete the loop and then repeat, bringing the end of the thread into the loop and around the string.

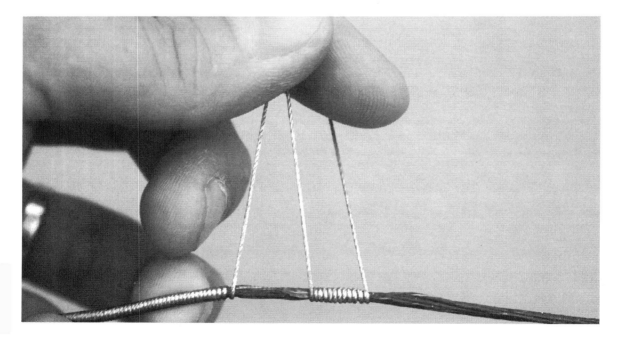

Continue wrapping backwards until you've covered 1/2 an inch. Make sure there is at least 1/2 an inch of empty space between the main serving and your little reverse wrap.

String Building - Endless Loop

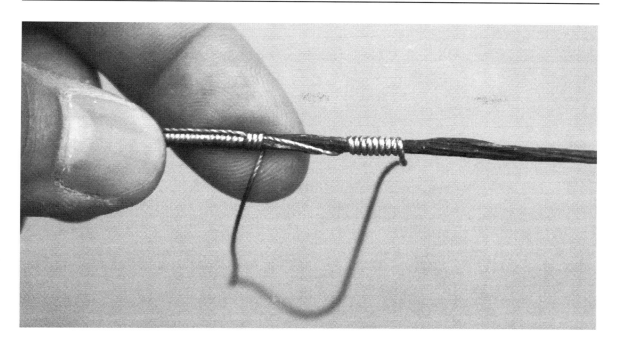

Lay the loose end of thread down under the loop and begin twisting the loop around. By bringing the loop around in the direction you wrapped, the thread will move from the little reverse wrap and on to the main wrap. Be sure to wrap as tightly as possible.

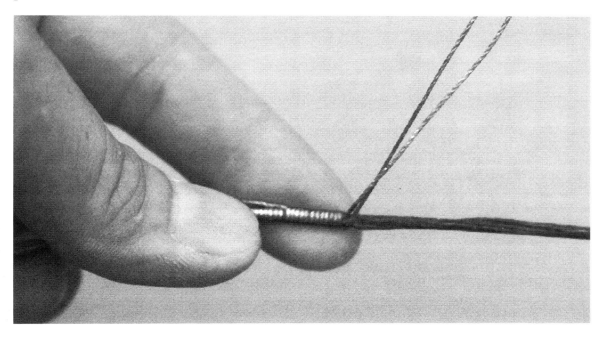

Once the wrap is completely moved over, straighten out the loop and make sure it isn't twisted or knotted as that will make the next step difficult.

Take-Down Archery

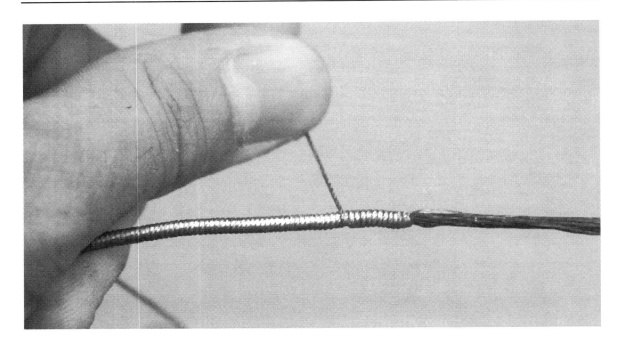

Pull the loose end through. This will secure the end of the serving and keep everything in place.

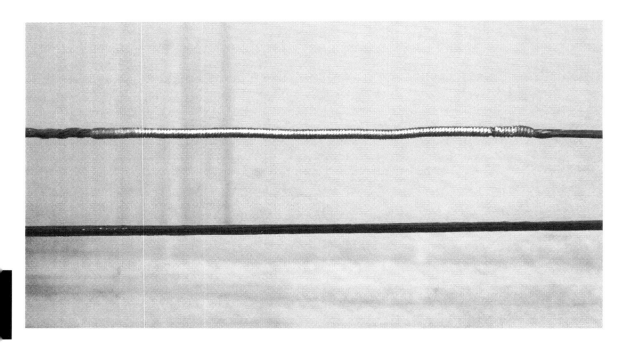

Trim the loose ends and place a drop of superglue on to both ends. This will help hold the thread in place and keep the string from pulling apart.

String Building - Endless Loop

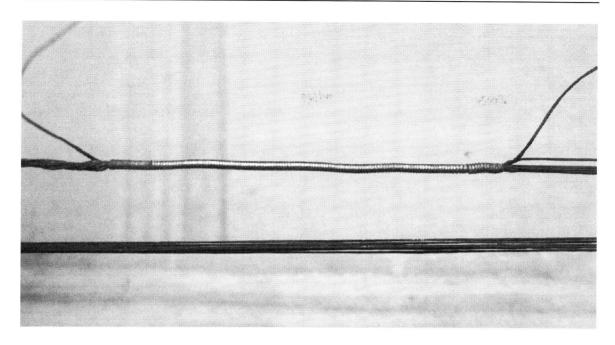

Untie the two loose strands of string material and pull them away from the main body of the string. Very carefully trim both loose strands, leaving both string bundles with the same number of strands. Repeat the whole serving process on the other bundle, starting 5 inches away from the third nail. (If the third nail is at 45 inches, start at 40 and serve toward the first nail)

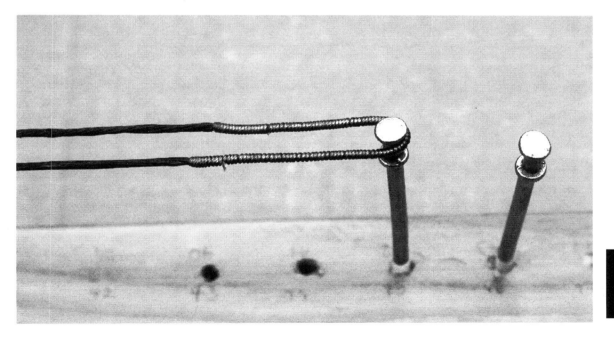

Once both bundles are served, slide the bundles around until the served ends rest on the nails. They should both rest fairly centered on the nails. One side may be a little longer and that is good, it will help the serving blend.

Take-Down Archery

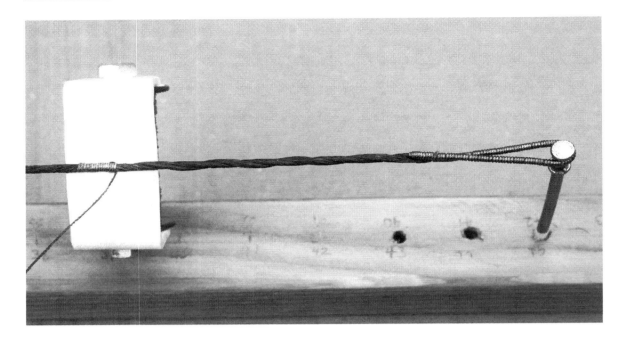

Start the serving about 6 inches away from the end of the loop. I personally like my end serving plus loop to equal 8 inches so that both loops and center serving are the same length. This can be as little as three inches long as still hold up.

Serve the end just as you did the loops, wrapping until 1/2 an inch needs to be wrapped.

String Building - Endless Loop

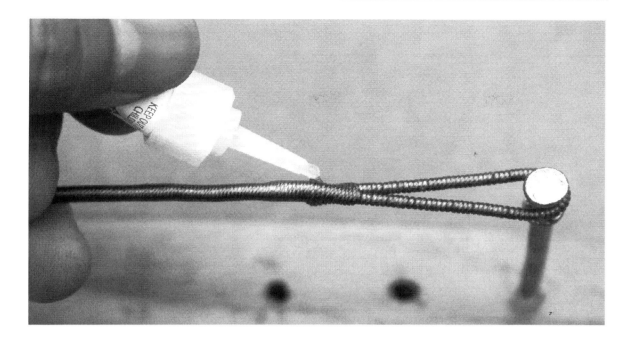

Complete the serving by doing the reverse-serve. A few drops of superglue will help keep the serving in place.

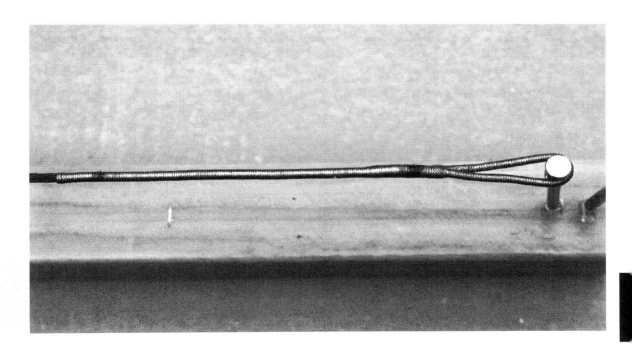

Here is the finished string loop. Repeat on the other string loop and the string is finished.

Take-Down Archery

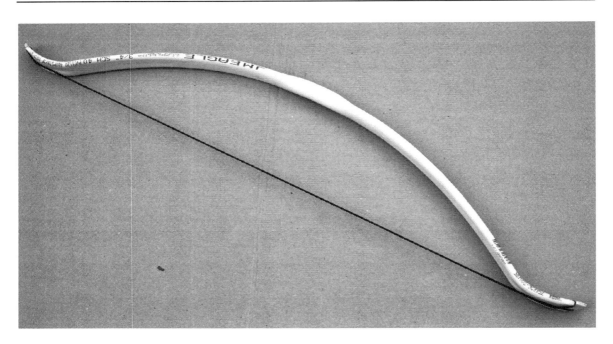

Congratulations on your completed endless loop string. Before placing the center serving, the string should be pre-stretched. To do this, place it on the bow it is made for and draw it a few times and leave it on the bow for a few hours. Alternatively, the string can be hung on a hook and about 20-50 pounds of weight can be suspended from the other side overnight. If the string stretches, it can be twisted to make it a little shorter.

Center Serving

One of the finishing touches before shooting a new string is to serve the center. A center serving will do a few things for a string. First, it will keep the string from fraying as the arrow's nock and your fingers constantly rub on the string. A smooth serving thread will also help with a smooth release and reduce wear on fingers, glove or release aid.

While the center serving can be done with the same material used for serving string loops, a monofilament or more durable thread would prolong the life of the serving. If your string is too thin, a thicker serving can help pad the string allowing arrow nocks to fit properly.

While most strings will last a while if shot without a center serving, it's always a good idea to put one on. It's easier to tell if a string is worn and needs to be replaced if there is a serving as the serving will usually wear down before the string breaks.

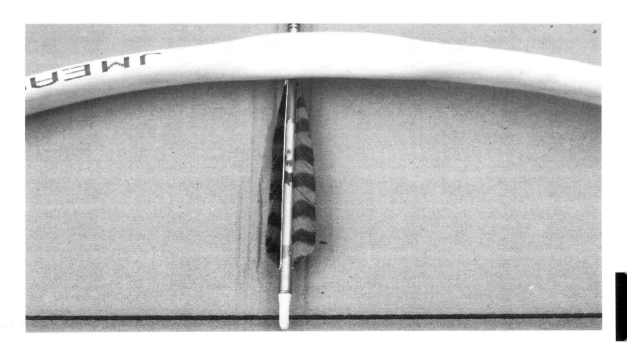

Begin by placing an arrow on the string as if you were to shoot. For starters, this should be about 1 to 2 inches away from the center of the handle. In the picture, the left side is the bow's upper limb and the right is the bow's lower limb.

Take-Down Archery

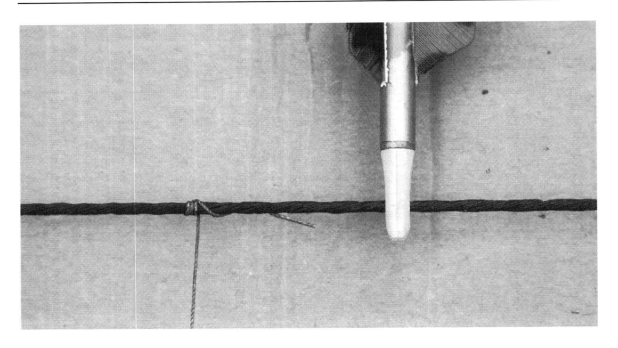

Begin your serving 2 inches above the nock of the arrow. If you use a release or shoot three fingers under, 1 inch above the nock is enough.

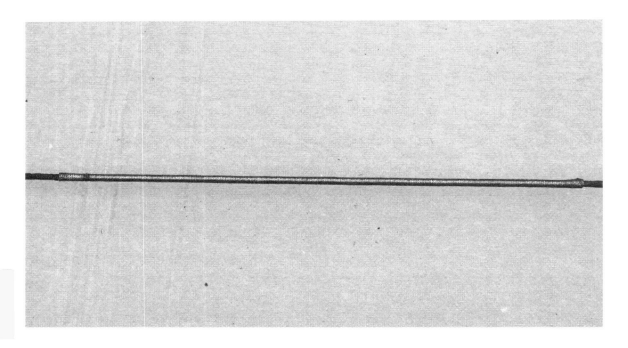

Continue wrapping for at least 6 inches. This will help protect the string from any abrasion that can come from an armguard, your arm and your fingers on the string. Finish off the serving and you are done.

Setting a Nock Point

One of the important aspects of consistent shooting is arrow placement. If you place the arrow on the string in the same spot every time, that is one less variable in your shooting. A nock point or nocking point is a small marker on the string that can be located by touch and feel. This allows the arrow to nock on to the string consistently.

Where the arrow goes on the string is important and can change the way an arrow flies. The simplest way to find a good nocking point is to simply shoot your bow. If the nocking point is too high to too low, the arrow will porpoise up and down. You can see how the arrow flies, and a good nocking point will ensure a clean up and down flight without porpoising.

A good starting point is to place the arrow on the rest and make a 90 degree angle with the string and arrow. Once you find that spot where your arrow fly true, mark it with a permanent marker right above the arrow's nock. After making sure that is the spot, you can set the nocking point.

There are little plastic and brass nocking points that can be purchased from most sporting goods and archery stores. In lieu of this, a simple nock point can be made with serving thread or any other light thread.

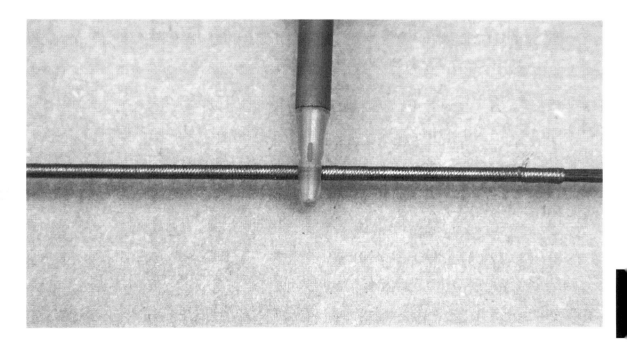

Set your arrow on the string where you normally shoot. Make sure to use arrow nocks that you normally use as different sized nocks will cause just a little bit of variation in arrow flight. The upper limb is on the right, the lower limb is on the left,

Take-Down Archery

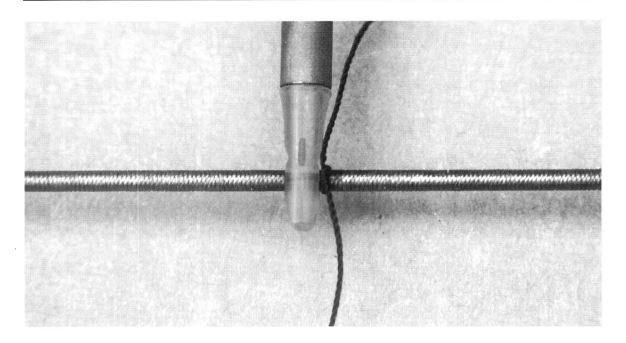

Take a length of thick thread or thin twine and tie a knot directly above the nock of the arrow. An overhand knot will secure the thread in place. Add a drop of superglue to the knot while pulling it taught.

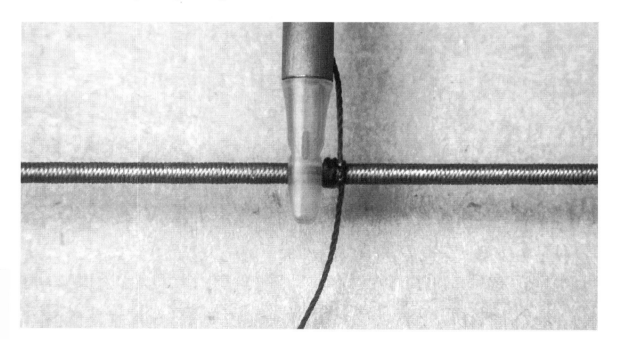

Tie another three overhand knots, alternating the side until you have a solid group of knots.

String Building - Setting a Nock Point

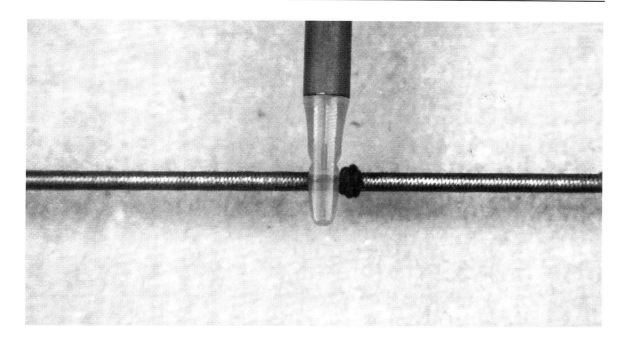

Tie one last knot backwards, over the other knots and saturate the thread in superglue. Once the glue sets, trim the loose ends and your nocking point is finished.

Gallery

Here are the three bows from this book, broken down. They each fit easily into these small containers with at least 3 arrow each.

Here are the bows out of their cases and fully assembled with arrows.

Gallery

The finished Tracker at full draw. The string angle is very close to being 90 degrees.

The finished Egyptian at full draw.

Take-Down Archery

The finished Nomad at full draw.

Heres the Nomad with its case and six arrows. The nomad fits very well in most standard camera tripod cases. The case also doubles as a back quiver that can hold a good number of arrows.

Gallery

At full draw with a release aid.

Shooting the Nomad from a strange twisted/kneeling position. You can see the arrows in the tripod case on my back. Behind me is a dense Hawaiian rainforest.

Take-Down Archery

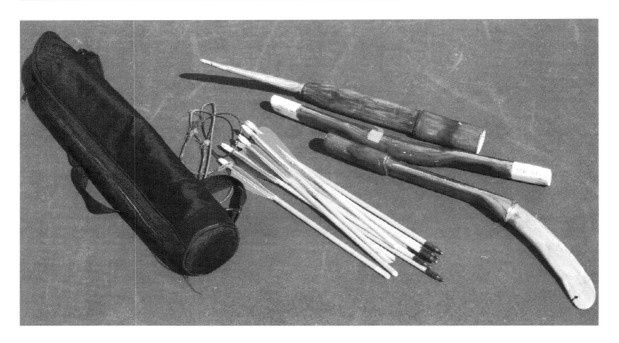

The basic contents of an archery bag. Your chosen case should be able to fit a good number of arrows, the bow and a string. Other optional items would be some string wax, spare arrow parts, a fletching jig, strings and material, a server and some extra release aids.

A set of 6 release aid templates. It's a good idea to transfer the designs on to card stock and cut them out. That way you can test to see which fits your hand the best.

Gallery

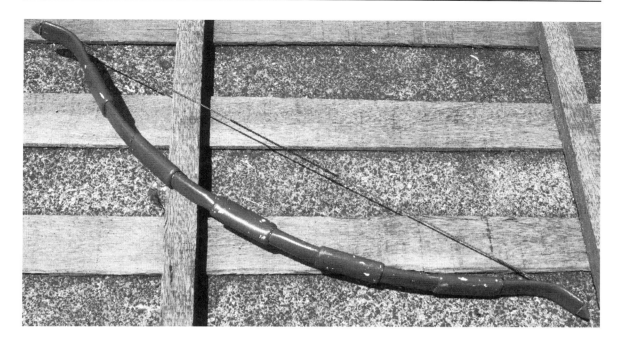

A 6 piece take down bow. This one pull 50 pounds at 28 inches and is slightly recurved. When broken down, the longest piece is under 9 inches long. While a little excessive, a very compact bow like this can be made. This bow is 5 months old and already has gone through 1,000 or more shots without fail.

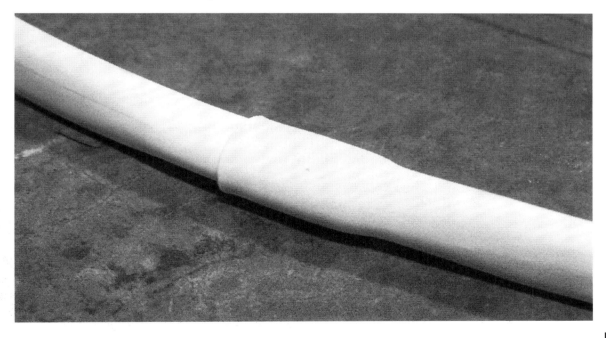

Another method of making a 2 piece take down in 1 inch pipe. Build your bow 4 inches longer than you need it to be and slide one side of the handle over the other. While this style works well, it is possible for the handle to snap just below where the pipe bulges. The inside piece needs to be rounded and very smooth.

Glossary

ABS - Acrylonitrile-Butadiene-Styrene, a plastic used often for plumbing applications as it is clean. It is also tough in cold temperatures.

Aluminum - A light and tough alloy of metal used often in modern arrows.

Anchor Point - The place where an arrow is drawn to before release every time.

AMO - The Archery Manufacturers and Merchants Organization, an old name for an organization that has set many standards for archery equipment.

AMO Length - The length of a bow as measured according to AMO standards. It also refers to a string that properly braces a bow of a labeled AMO length, regardless of true bow length.

Archer - A practitioner of archery, a user of the bow and arrow.

Archer's Paradox - The effect of an arrow traveling along the path of the string rather than the line of the arrow.

Arrow - The projectile used in archery, fired from a bow.

Arrow Pass - The place on a bow where the arrow is placed and passes over when fired.

Arrow Rest - A shelf or similar device that holds an arrow onto the handle during the draw cycle.

ATA - The Archery Trade Association, the current name for the AMO.

Back - The side of the bow that faces away from the archer.

Belly - The side of the bow that faces the archer.

Bow - A weapon that uses spring-like limbs to propel an arrow.

Bowfishing - Using a bow to harvest fish above and below water.

Bowhunting - Hunting game animals using a bow and arrow.

Bow String - A strong and ideally inelastic cord that connects the tips of a bow and allows a bow to fire arrows.

Bowyer - A person who build bows.

Brace - Either a bow when it is strung, or the act of stringing a bow.

Brace Height - The distance between the handle of a bow and the string when the bow is at brace.

Carbon Fiber - A lightweight material composed of carbon fibers in a matrix of resin that is very tough and used in modern arrows.

Centershot - A bow that is incredibly accurate by reducing the effect of archer's paradox.

Collapse - A condition where a bow folds in an area due to lost strength.

Composite Bow - A bow made up of different materials fixed together.

Compound Bow - A modern bow that uses a system of cables and pulleys or cams to increase efficiency.

Compression - A crushing, pushing force that the belly of a bow undergoes.

Deflex - A bend in a bow that goes away from the archer.

Glossary

Drawing - Pulling a bow back in order to store energy and prepare for the release.

Draw Length - Either the maximum length a bow can be pulled to or the length an archer pulls their bow to.

Draw Weight - How much force is required to pull a bow to full draw, usually measured in pounds.

Dry Fire - Also called a dry release or dry loose, it is drawing and releasing a bow without an arrow on the string.

Fiberglass - Glass fibers in a matrix of resin, a tough composite used regularly for both modern bows and arrows.

Field Archery - Shooting at targets of unknown distances in a field or open space.

Flatten Taper - A taper in a pipe or cylinder formed by flattening one side progressively more than the other, forming a smooth taper.

Fletching - The feathers or vanes that stabilize and arrow in flight.

Flex - The amount something is capable of bending.

Handle - The center portion of a bow that the archer holds.

Heat Gun - A device that uses a heating element combined with a fan or blower to deliver hot air.

Horse Archer - An archer who shoots from horseback. Also known as a mounted archer.

Horse Bow - A bow used on horseback. Usually refers to shorter Asiatic composite bows.

Laminated Bow - A bow made of different pieces glued together. It may be pieces of one material or many different materials.

Limb - The flexible arms of a bow.

Mounted Archery - The sport of shooting a bow from horseback.

Nock - Can refer to the point on a bow where the string attaches, the notch at the end of an arrow where it attaches to the string, or the act of attaching an arrow to the bowstring.

Nock to Nock - NTN, The length of a bow measured from the bottom of one nock to the other.

Off Center - A bow that does not allow an arrow to rest near the center line of the bow.

Off the Hand - Shooting a bow without a rest, the arrow rests on the bow hand.

Past Center - A bow that allows an arrow to sit perfectly centered because the bow is aligned off to the side of center.

PE - Polyethylene, a common plastic used for food and water storage as well as piping for potable water.

Poundage - Another term for draw weight as measured in pounds.

PP - Polypropylene, a tough plastic used for ropes, plumbing pipes and joints that need to be flexed repeatedly without failing.

PVC - Polyvinyl Chloride, a common plastic that is used for many different purposes such as clothing, construction and plumbing. It is hard and brittle in its pure form.

PVC Pipe - Plastic piping used for plumbing, drainage, wiring housing and transport of corrosive fluids.

Quill - The hard, fingernail like main shaft of an arrow, also called the rachis.

Recurve - A curve in the tips of a bow that face away from the archer. A recurve is a type of reflex. Can also be a bow that is recurved.

Release - Can be the act of firing a bow by letting go of the string, a style of letting the arrow go or a mechanical aid for drawing and releasing a bow.

Reflex - A curve in a bow that faces away from the archer.

Riser - Center portion of a bow that contains the handle and arrow pass. It fades into the limbs on either side.

Selfbow - A bow made of one material, usually of wood.

Siyah - The static tips or ears on an Asiatic composite bow.

Spine - The measure of how much an arrow can resist bending and flexing.

Static Recurve - A recurve that does not move or bend during the draw.

Stave - A single piece of material used to make a bow, usually a strip of wood.

Stickbow - A bow, regardless of material, that does not make use of sights or other aids. One exception is the use of an arrow rest or shelf. Called a stickbow because it's "just a stick and a string".

String Bridge - A place on a siyah where the bowstring sits and tracks.

String Length - The length of a string from loop to loop. It is usually 3 to 4 inches shorter than the bow's ntn length. Not to be confused with AMO length which is the approximate length of a bow.

Take Down - A style of bow that breaks down into smaller pieces for ease of storage and transport.

Taper Flattening - The act of flattening something with a taper in thickness from one end to the other.

Target Archery - Shooting at fixed targets at known distances.

Tension - A pulling force that affects the back of a bow.

Tiller - A tool used to establish the flex of a bow, the flex of a bow or the difference between flex in the top and bottom limbs.

Thickness Taper - The taper in thickness in a bow limb.

Traditional Archery - A term that usually excludes compound bows and other modern mechanical bows while including longbows and recurve bows. The term can range from the use of only natural material equipment all the way to solely man-made materials as long as compounds aren't used.

UV Light - A form of radiation that can damage polymers by breaking bonds. It can cause plastic polymers like PVC to discolor and grow brittle over time.

Web - Also called the barbs of a feather, the main body of a feather that consists of individual branches that connect together.

Working Recurve - A recurve that bends or unfurls as the bow is drawn.

Bonus Track : Part One
ABS Stalker Quiver

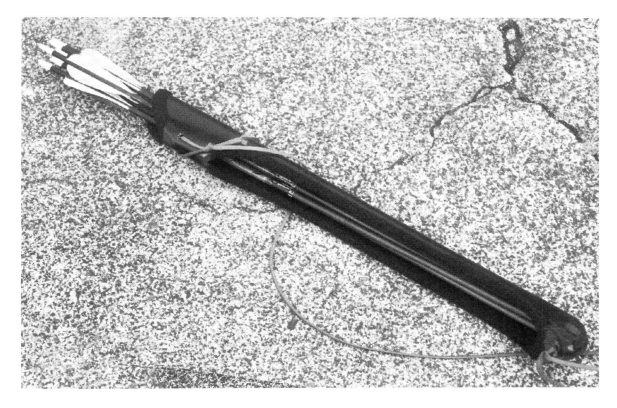

One of the things that really helps when out at the range or in the field is something to hold your arrows for you. There are a lot of quiver styles out there, plenty that can be made from plastic piping. This one is one of my favorites, great for carrying around up to 9 arrows with field points or 6 with broadheads or blunt tips.

It's a simple design, essentially a tube with a closed end and a large opening in the side. It's pretty versatile and can be worn off the shoulder, on the back, tied to a belt or around the shoulders. Arrows can be drawn from the top of the quiver or from the side.

While it may seem awkward at first, drawing arrows from the side saves a lot of movement and is usually a little quieter than drawing out the top. This is especially true of broadheads and blunts. Since you draw forward instead of back or behind, there is a lot less wasted motion and an arrow can be drawn quickly and without a lot of room.

The pipe used for quivers like this can either be cellular core or thin wall pipe, PVC or ABS. In the US, cellular core ABS is usually easy to find. Cellular core pipe is basically a plastic foam sandwiched between two thin layers of solid plastic.

Take-Down Archery

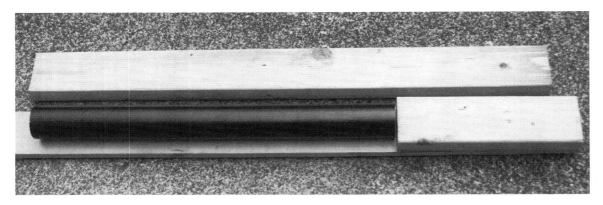

Start with your pipe on top of your flattening jig with a 2x4 on one side. This will become the mouth of the quiver. The pipe should be cellular core PVC, ABS or thin-wall PVC. Schedule 40 will work but will be heavy and won't form properly. Start with 24 inches of pipe or 4 inches shorter than your arrows.

The 2x4 should be about an inch or so shorter than the pipe. If using 3 inch pipe, a 2x4 plus a 1x2 should give the height you need to make the mouth the right width.

Heat up the top 5 inches of the pipe and partially flatten it so that it tapers from full thickness to the height of the 2x4 at the mouth.

Bonus Track Part One - ABS Stalker Quiver

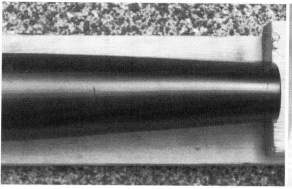

This is what the mouth of the quiver should look like.

Take the other end and heat up around 3 inches. Crimp the pipe as much as you can with a hot pad or heat resistant glove.

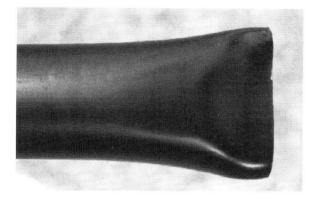

Cellular core and thin-wall pipe is very flexible when heated, so it will be easy to form this into the quiver bottom later. If using schedule 40 PVC, The base of the crimp will become the base of the quiver.

Cut out the outline of the quiver. The bottom will curve slightly. Start at the bottom for cellular pipe. Start right where the pipe is crimped to maximize quiver space for solid. The top curve should be the same depth as the width of the mouth. The center cut out starts 2 inches from the bottom and three inches in from the top and curves to half the width of the pipe.

Take-Down Archery

Sand and round all the sharp edges and refine the shape of the quiver at this point.

Heat the bottom of the quiver gently until it is pliable. Quickly press the seam together from both sides.

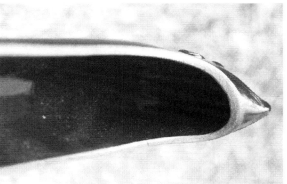

This rounds out the bottom of the quiver and fives the arrows space to sit. This type of shaping can only be done with cellular core and thin wall pipe.

The bottom should be rounded out like this.

To make the quiver slimmer, gently heat the center portion and then press it together slightly so that the quiver all lines up.

Bonus Track Part One - ABS Stalker Quiver

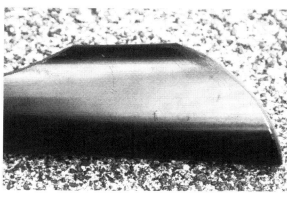

Heat up the section of quiver between the mouth and side opening. Pinch it to create a ridge.

Drill a 1/4 inch hole through the top of the quiver, at least 1/4 of an inch away from the ridge and mouth of the quiver.

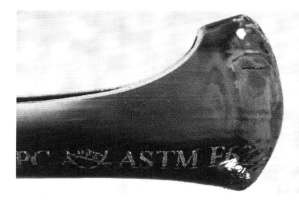

Drill another 1/4 inch hole at the base of the quiver, about 1/4 inch away from the edge.

Cut a strip of adhesive backed hook and loop fastener. This is the loop or fuzzy side.

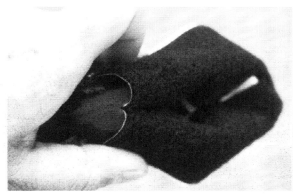

To determine how long of a strip you'll need, fold it so it goes inside the mouth of the quiver like this.

Cut three triangles out of the strip, leaving a top edge that will be the trim on the outside of the quiver. Curve the top edges as well.

Take-Down Archery

Fold the strip over and test-fit before removing the backing.

Work a little at a time, removing the backing as you go. Start from the inside, making sure the lines match.

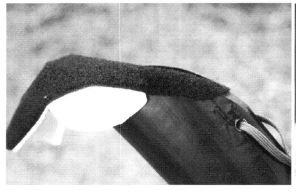

Smooth over the outside trim as you go along.

Remove more backing and continue covering the mouth of the quiver.

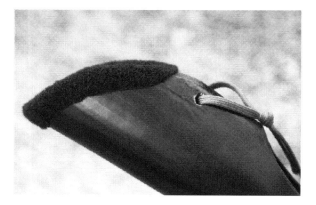

The mouth of the quiver completed.

Bonus Track Part One - ABS Stalker Quiver

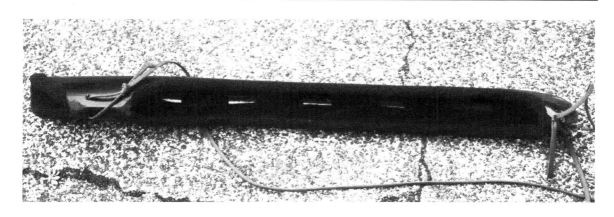

In a similar fashion, line the inside and edges of the quiver with the same material. An alternative would be leather, felt or fur. This is to help keep arrows from rattling around and making noise.

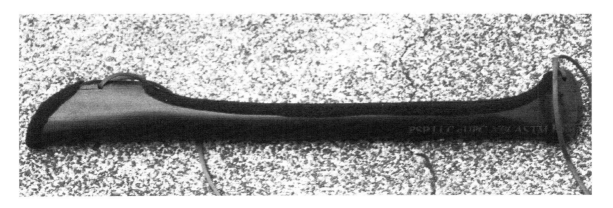

Here's the completed quiver, ready for use. The strap simply ties on to the top and bottom strap holes. An old bag strap or leather belt can make a good strap as will a length of paracord or similar rope.

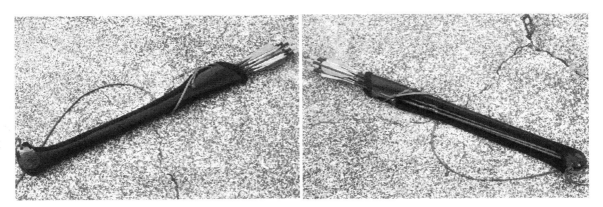

To retrieve arrows from the quiver, either pull them from the mouth of the quiver like a normal belt or back quiver or from the side opening. To do this, grab an arrow near the point, slide it up to clear the bottom of the quiver and then push the arrow forward and out. This motion require a lot less movement and can be done in cramped spaces.

Bonus Track : Part Two
Screw-In Wood Adapter

    There are a lot of choices in the world and sometimes I wish there weren't so many things to have to decide upon. In the context of wooden arrows, deciding between field points, target points, blunts and broadheads can be challenging. Add this to the fact that these parts cannot be easily changed from arrow to arrow, you're going to need a really big quiver to carry all your different shafts.

    To trim down on space one could carry a few good shafts and a nice selection of points for each. This is what I do with aluminum and carbon arrows to save space as well as use the same shafts for target shooting and field use. With a little modification, this can be done with wooden arrows as well.

    We'll be using a piece of aluminum arrow with a point insert over the front of a wood arrow shaft. This will allow screw-in points to fit onto the end of wooden arrows, allowing you to carry a few arrows and a good set of different points.

    This isn't a perfect way to do this and does add a bit of weight to the arrow, so choose points accordingly.

Bonus Track Part Two - Screw-In Wood Adapter

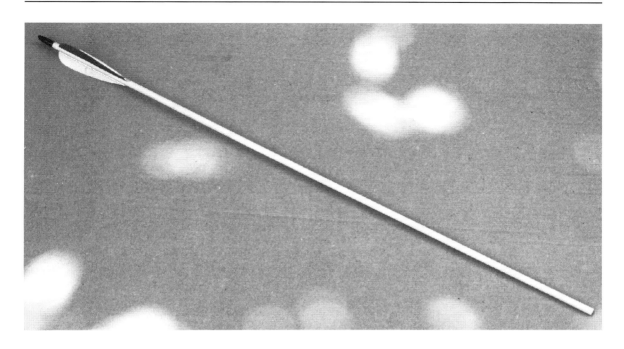

Start with a wooden arrow shaft. This works best with 5/16 inch shafts, though can work with 11/32 and 3/8 inch as well.

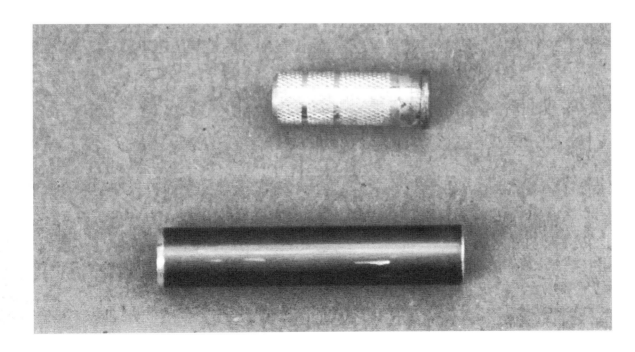

Cut a 2 inch length of 2216 aluminum arrow shaft. Bevel the ends, making sure to really taper the back edge. You will also need a screw-in insert for the 2216 arrow.

Take-Down Archery

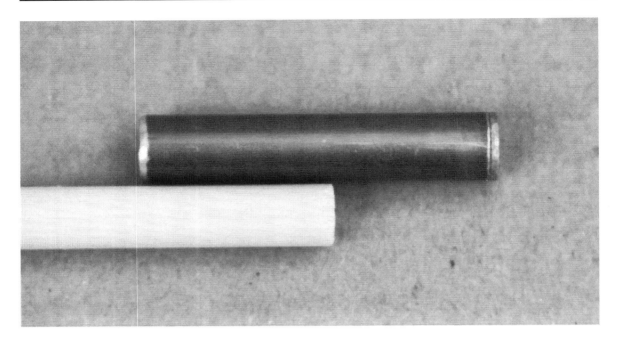

Glue the insert into the front of the aluminum arrow shaft. Most inserts are 3/4 to 1 inch long, so measure the inside of the aluminum shaft behind the insert. If your wooden arrow is thicker than 5/16 inches, you will need to cut a slight tenon. This can easily be done with a file and sandpaper.

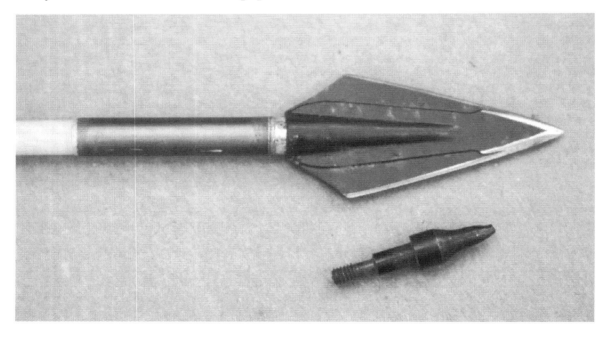

Glue the aluminum arrow shaft on to the wood arrow, completing the point. Here are a couple of points that can be used. If you plan on using broadheads, you will want to make sure to screw in the broadhead and get it lined up where you want it before gluing the point assembly on to the arrow as it will be difficult to align it later.

Bonus Track Part Two - Screw-In Wood Adapter

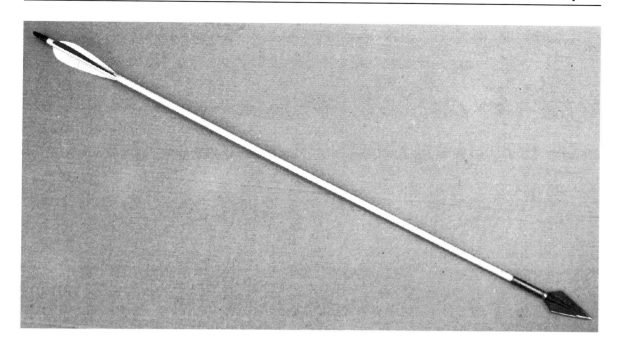

Here's the finished point assembly. Now this wood arrow can take any standard archery point as well as any homemade points using an 8-32 threaded screw or rod.

If you've ever wanted to build a wooden bow, check out
The Backyard Bowyer : The Beginner's Guide to Building Bows

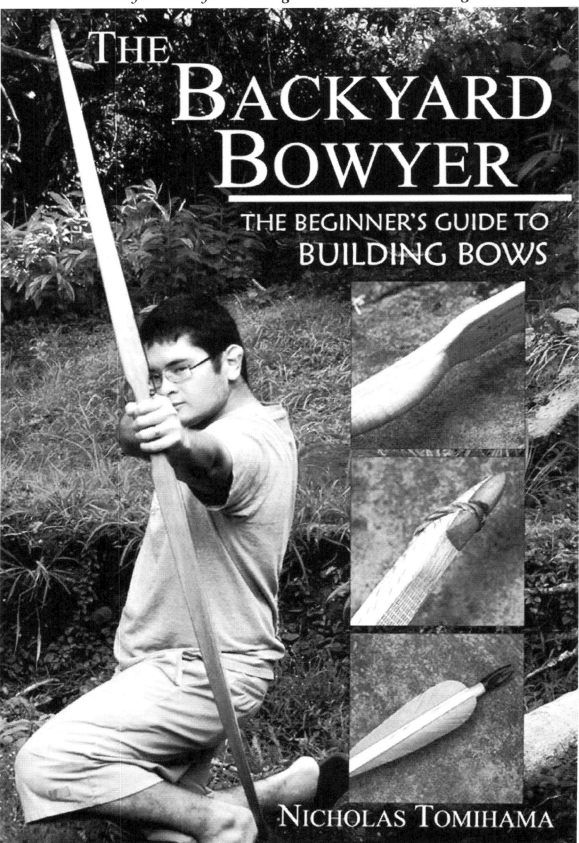

Made in the USA
Lexington, KY
09 November 2015